DESI KHANA

The Best Of
Indian Vegetarian Cooking

∾ TARLA DALAL ∾

Tenth Printing : 2000

Price Rs. 215/-

Published & Distributed by :

Sanjay & Company,

353, A-1, Shah & Nahar Industrial Estate, Dhanraj Mill Compound,
Lower Parel(W), Mumbai - 400 013. INDIA.
Tel. :(91-22) 496 8068 Fax : (91-22) 496 5876 E-mail : sanjay@tarladalal.com

Printed by : **Jupiter Prints,** Mumbai

: Designed by :   : Photographs by :
Mr. Niranjan Kamatkar   Mr. Mahesh Hiremath

: Food Stylist :
Mr. Suzanne Merwanji

ISBN No. 81-86469-00-1

Visit us on our Home Page http://www.tarladalal.com

BY THE SAME AUTHOR

OTHER BOOKS BY TARLA DALAL

WESTERN COOKING
The Chocolate Cook Book
Eggless Desserts
Mocktails & Snacks
Soups & Salads
Mexican Cooking
Easy Gourmet Cooking

INDIAN COOKING
Tava Cooking
Rotis & Subzis
The Complete Gujarati Cook Book
Mithai

HEALTH COOKING
Low Calorie Healthy Cooking
Eat Your Way To Good Health

EASTERN COOKING
ChineseCooking
Thai Cooking

GENERAL COOKING
Mixer Cook Book
Pleasures of Vegetarian Cooking
Delights of Vegetarian Cooking
Joys of Vegetarian Cooking
Cooking With Kids

Exciting Vegetarian Cooking
Party Cooking
Microwave Cooking
Quick & Easy Cooking
Saatvik Khana

MINI SERIES
A new world of Idlis & Dosas
Cooking under 10 minutes
Pizzas and Pastas
Fun Food for Children
Roz Ka Khana

3

AUTHOR ON THE BOOK

India is a vast and varied land; and not surprisingly, the variation and diversity is reflected in the different styles and practices of cooking. Moreover, a significant proportion of the population being vegetarian, India has no equal in the field of vegetarian cooking.

With changing times, there have been continuing changes in the kitchen size and its equipment on the one hand and in taste and diet preferences on the other. This is naturally more pronounced in the urban areas where the housewife is hardpressed for time, for space and for help. Elaborate cooking methods like those of the maharajas or those used in Moghlai and Nawabi cuisines are just not practical anymore. Accordingly, my emphasis has been on simple recipes which can be prepared in reasonable time. And whilst catering to the Indian weakness for rich dishes and sweets, I have borne in mind present-day medical and nutritional advice and kept the extent of fats used in cooking to the minimum.

In this selection of *desi* recipes, I have tried to place before you dishes which are Indian but at the same time different from the usual run and dishes which keep in mind the needs of good health.

I wish you happy cooking and eating.

CONTENTS

5

DESI JAL-PAAN

(Drinks/Sharbats)

These drinks are specially created from
exotic *desi* ingredients like Saffron, Khas,
Chandan (Sandalwood), Kewra and Coconut.
They are easy to prepare and have unique
flavours of their own.

LIME CUP

Lemon juice, rose syrup and ginger transform sweet lime juice into a delectable drink.

Preparation time : a few minutes. No cooking. Serves 6.

5 teacups sweets lime juice
2 tablespoons rose syrup
4 teaspoons lemon juice
1 teaspoon ginger juice
crushed ice

Mix all the ingredients except the ice.

▶ **Serve in tall glasses with crushed ice** ◀

COCONUT KEWRA DRINK

Picture on page 17

A refreshing coconut drink with a unique flavour of kewra.

Preparation time : a few minutes. No cooking. Serves 4.

4 teacups coconut water
4 tablespoons coconut cream (meat), cut into pieces
4 tablespoons kewra syrup
rose petals
crushed ice

Mix all the ingredients except the ice.

▶ **Serve with crushed ice** ◀

MANGO DRINK

Picture on page 17

A tasty trio of lemon, mango and saffron.

Preparation time : a few minutes. No cooking. Serves 4.

juice of 4 lemons
12 teaspoons sugar
4 pinches saffron
8 tablespoons mango (Alphonso) juice
mango slices
crushed ice

Mix all the ingredients with 4 teacups of water.

▶ **Serve with crushed ice** ◀

KHUS DRINK

Picture on page 17

A refreshing drink for the hot summer.

Preparation time: a few minutes. No cooking. Serves 4.

16 teaspoons khus syrup
4 tablespoons soaked takmaria (sabja) seeds
16 teaspoons kewra water (optional)
a few drops lemon juice
3 bottles lemon drink
crushed ice.

Mix all the ingredients except the ice.

▶ **Serve in tall glasses with crushed ice** ◀

SAFFRON SANDALWOOD DRINK

Picture on page 94

Sandalwood gives this sherbet a pleasant cooling effect.

Preparation time : a few minutes. No cooking. Serves 6.

2 pinches saffron
4 tablespoons lemon juice
6 tablespoons sugar
1/4 teaspoon cardamom powder
1 1/2 teaspoons sandalwood paste
1/4 teaspoon salt
crushed ice

For the sandalwood paste
sandalwood
a little water

For the sandalwood paste
Rub sandalwood with a little water in a pestle and mortar or on a flat surface.

How to proceed
1. Heat the saffron in a small bowl with a little warm water and rub until it dissolves.
2. Transfer the saffron water to a larger bowl and add 5 teacups of water with all the remaining ingredients except the ice.

▶ **Pour into glasses and serve with crushed ice** ◀

KHANE-SE-PEHELE

(Shorbas/Soups)

You will find these unusual and typically
Indian flavoured soups a welcome change
from Western soups. The delicate use of
spices like cumin seeds, a dash of green chilli
etc. in combination with fresh herbs, lentils
and vegetables imparts special aromas to
these soups and makes them a perfect match
for *desi* khana.

CURD SHORBA

Picture on page 18

Wholesome curd kadhi transformed into a light and refreshing soup.

Preparation time : 15 minutes. Cooking time : 10 minutes. Serves 6.

2 teacups fresh curds
2 teaspoons gram flour (besan)
2 tablespoons milk
½ teaspoon cumin seeds
½ onion, chopped (optional)
2 green chillies, chopped
½ teaspoon grated ginger

2 tablespoons chopped tomato
a pinch turmeric powder
2 tablespoons chopped cucumber
2 tablespoons ghee
salt to taste
1 tablespoon chopped coriander
for garnishing

1. Beat the curds, gram flour and milk.
2. Heat the ghee and fry the cumin seeds until they begin to crackle.
Add the onion, green chillies and ginger and fry again for a few seconds.
3. Add the curd mixture, turmeric powder and salt.
4. Add the tomato and cucumber and give one boil.

▶ **Sprinkle coriander on top and serve hot** ◀

TOMATO SHORBA

A lovely soup from Maharashtra made from tomatoes and coconut with a delicate touch of spices.

Preparation time : 15 minutes. Cooking time : 15 minutes. Serves 6.

1 kg. tomatoes
2 teaspoons gram flour (besan)
½ coconut, grated
1 teaspoon cumin seeds
3 to 4 curry leaves
2 to 3 slit green chillies

1 tablespoon jaggery or
2 teaspoons sugar
1 tablespoon ghee
salt to taste
1 tablespoon chopped coriander
for garnishing

1. Cut the tomatoes into big pieces. Add 2 teacups of water and put to cook. When cooked, prepare a thick purée by passing through a sieve.
2. Add 2½ teacups of water to the grated coconut and blend in a liquidiser. Strain and take out thin coconut milk.
3. Add the gram flour to the coconut milk and mix well.
4. Heat the ghee and fry the cumin seeds for a few seconds. Add the curry leaves, green chillies and fry again for a few seconds.
5. Add the tomato purée, coconut milk mixture, jaggery and salt.
6. Cook for a few minutes.

▶ **Sprinkle corainder on top and serve hot** ◀

HERB SOUP

Picture on page 18

A refreshing soup using fresh herbs and mild spices.

Preparation time : 10 minutes. Cooking time : 30 minutes. Serves 6.

1 teacup finely chopped spinach
3 spring onions, finely chopped
1 tablespoon chopped coriander
6 mint leaves (optional)
1 level tablespoon plain flour (maida)

2 pinches nutmeg powder
6 black pepper, ground
3 tablespoons fresh cream
1 tablespoon butter
salt to taste

1. Boil the spinach, onions, coriander and mint leaves in 5 teacups of water until soft.
2. Blend the mixture in a liquidiser and prepare a thick purée.
3. Melt the butter, add the flour and cook on a slow flame until froth appears, while stirring throughout.
4. Add the purée, ground spices and salt and simmer for 10 minutes.
5. Beat the cream and add to the soup.

▶ **Serve hot** ◀

PANEER

And

DAL SOUP

Highly nutritious.

Preparation time : 10 minutes. Cooking time : 25 minutes. Serves 6.

2 tablespoons moong dal
100 grams paneer,
cut into thin strips
1 teacup finely chopped spinach

1 onion, chopped
1½ tablespoons butter
salt and pepper to taste
oil for deep frying

1. Cook the moong dal, spinach and onion in 6 teacups of water
   When cooked, blend the mixture in a liquidiser.
2. Strain the soup and add the butter, salt and pepper.
3. Deep fry the paneer lightly and add to the soup.

▶ Serve hot ◀

CORN

And

DAL SOUP

Colourful and tasty. If fresh corn is not available, use one small can of corn instead.

Preparation time : 15 minutes. Cooking time : 25 minutes. Serves 6.

2 tender corncobs, grated
1 tablespoon moong dal
1 onion, chopped
1 tablespoon finely
chopped celery
1 tomato, chopped

1 level tablespoon cornflour
3 tablespoons finely chopped spinach
3 tablespoons tomato ketchup (optional)
1 teaspoon lemon juice
1 tablespoon butter
salt and pepper to taste

From left to right : Coconut Kewra Drink–*Page 10* ,
Khus Drink–*Page 11*, Mango Drink–*Page 11*.

To serve
grated cheese

1. Cook the corn and moong dal in 5 teacups of water until tender.
2. Melt the butter and fry the onion and celery for 1 minute.
3. Add the cooked corn with its liquid and the tomato.
4. Mix the cornflour with a little water and add to the soup. Boil for 10 minutes.
5. Add the spinach, tomato ketchup and lemon juice.
6. Add salt and pepper.

▶ **Serve hot with grated cheese** ◀

COCO PEANUT SOUP

Coconut, milk and peanuts give you this tasty mild-flavoured soup.

Preparation time : 10 minutes. Cooking time : 5 minutes. Serves 6.

1 large coconut, grated
3 teaspoons gram flour (besan)
½ teaspoon cumin seeds
1 green chilli, chopped
2 tablespoons finely
chopped cucumber
2 tablespoons finely
chopped tomatoes

2 tablespoons peanuts,
coarsely powdered
1 tablespoon ghee
salt to taste
1 tablespoon fresh coriander
for garnishing

1. Add 5 teacups of water to the grated coconut and blend in a liquidiser. Strain.
2. Add the gram flour to the coconut milk and mix well.
3. Heat the ghee and fry the cumin seeds until they begin to crackle.
4. Add the green chilli and fry again for a few seconds.
5. Add the coconut milk and boil for 1 minute while stirring throughout.
6. Add the cucumber, tomatoes and peanuts and boil for 1 minute. Add the salt.

▶ **Sprinkle coriander on top and serve hot** ◀

MULLIGATAWNY SOUP

A *variation of the popular South Indian soup.*

Preparation time : 20 minutes. Cooking time : 30 minutes. Serves 8.

For the powdered masala

2 teaspoons
coriander seeds
2 teaspoons
cumin seeds
2 teaspoons
aniseeds (saunf)
¼ teaspoon fenugreek
(methi) seeds
2 small sticks
cinnamon

For the soup

1 coconut, grated
2 onions, chopped
2 carrots, chopped
12 mm. piece ginger
4 cloves garlic, finely chopped
150 grams masoor dal or toovar dal
3 large tomatoes, chopped
¼ teaspoon turmeric powder
3 tablespoons cooked rice
lemon juice to taste
2 tablespoons oil
salt to taste

For the powdered masala

1. Roast without oil the coriander seeds, cumin seeds, aniseeds, fenugreek seeds and cinnamon sticks in a hot tawa (griddle) for 2 to 3 minutes. Cool.
2. Grind into a fine powder.

For the soup

1. Add 1 teacup of water to the grated coconut and blend in a liquidiser. Strain and take out thick coconut milk.
2. Heat the oil and fry the onions, carrots, ginger and garlic for 2 minutes.
3. Add the dal, tomatoes, powdered masala, turmeric powder and 5 teacups of water. Cover and cook for 15 minutes or until the vegetables are soft. When cooked, blend the mixture in a liquidiser. Strain.
4. Add the coconut milk, rice, lemon juice and salt.

▶ **Serve hot** ◀

DESI CHAATKAR

(Raitas/Chutneys/Salads)

Desi meals are truly not complete
without accompaniments like raitas,
chutneys etc. A traditional meal would
be accompanined by 2 to 3 types of
chutneys, pickles and papads.

FRUIT
And
VEGETABLE RAITA

Picture on page 84

Sweet, sour and slightly pungent.

Preparation time : 10 minutes. No cooking. Serves 6.

1½ teacups thick fresh curds
2 tablespoons fresh cream
1 teaspoon mustard powder
1 teaspoon cumin seeds
3 tablespoons grapes

1 cucumber, chopped
2 apples, chopped
1 banana, sliced
2 teaspoons sugar
salt to taste

1. Mix the curds, cream, mustard powder, cumin seeds, sugar, and salt. Chill for ½ hour.
2. Add the fruits and cucumber and mix well.

▶ **Serve cold** ◀

SPINACH RAITA

A raita with the goodness of spinach.

Preparation time : a few minutes. Cooking time : a few minutes. Serves 6.

2 teacups spinach leaves
2½ teacups fresh curds
½ green chilli, chopped
2 pinches pepper powder

2 pinches sugar
a little chilli powder
(for sprinkling)
salt to taste

1. Steam the spinach leaves for a few minutes. Squeeze out the water and chop finely.
2. Beat the curds and add the green chilli, pepper, sugar and salt. Mix well.
3. Add the spinach and mix well.
4. Sprinkle chilli powder on top.

▶ **Serve cold** ◀

BEETROOT CUCUMBER

And

TOMATO RAITA

An everyday raita.

Preparation time : 15 minutes. Cooking time : 1 minute. Serves 6.

2 teacups fresh curds
1 beetroot, boiled and cut into cubes
2 cucumbers, cut into cubes
2 tomatoes, chopped
3 tablespoons roughly
chopped peanuts

2 tablespoons chopped coriander
1 teaspoon chopped green chillies
2 tablespoons grated fresh
or flaked coconut
1 teaspoon sugar
salt to taste

For the tempering
1 teaspoon cumin seeds
2 pinches asafoetida
2 teaspoons oil

1. Beat the curds and add all the remaining ingredients.
2. Prepare the tempering by heating the oil and frying
the cumin seeds until they begin to crackle. Then add the asafoetida.
3. Pour the tempering over the raita.

▶ **Serve cold** ◀

KHATTI MEETHI

FRUIT CHUTNEY

Sweet and sour tastes great with savouries.

Preparation time : 15 minutes. No cooking. Serves 10.

2 pineapple slices or
4 tablespoons chopped pineapple
2 bananas, sliced
2 guavas, chopped

1 pear, chopped
black and green grapes
2 apples, chopped
2 teacups sweet chutney, page 24

23

1. Chop all the fruits finely.
2. Add to the chutney and mix.

▶ **Use as required** ◀

FRUIT CHUTNEY

Yet another popular sweet and sour chutney.

Preparation time : 10 minutes. Cooking time : 10 minutes. Makes about 300 ml.

3 tablespoons
tamarind water, (page 73, step 4) or paste
3 tablespoons sugar
1 teacup mixed
chopped fruits

1 teaspoon chilli powder
1 teaspoon roasted
cumin seed powder
1/2 teaspoon black salt (sanchal)
salt to taste

1. Mix the tamarind paste, sugar and 1 teacup water and put to boil.
Boil for 3 minutes, then remove from the heat.
2. Add the fruit, chilli powder, cumin seed powder, black salt and salt.

▶ **Serve cold** ◀

SWEET CHUTNEY

Serve with fried snacks and chaat.

Preparation time : 5 minutes. Cooking time : 7 minutes. Makes 1 1/2 cups.

175 grams dates
50 grams tamarind
1/2 teaspoon cumin seeds

1/2 teaspoon chilli powder
1/2 teaspoon black salt (sanchal)
salt to taste

1. Remove seeds from the tamarind and dates and wash them.
Add 1 teacup of water and keep aside. After 2 hours, cook for 5 minutes.
2. Blend in a liquidiser and strain.
3. Roast the cumin seeds until they begin to crackle. Pound into a coarse powder.
4. Add the chilli powder, cumin seed powder, black salt and salt
to the tamarind-date purée and mix well.

▶ **Use as required** ◀

COCONUT CHUTNEY

Picture on page 93

Goes well with South Indian snacks.

Preparation time : 5 minutes. Cooking time : 2 minutes. Makes 1 cup.

4 tablespoons grated coconut
4 tablespoons roasted
  gram dal (dalia)
3 small green chillies
2 tablespoons chopped coriander
2 curry leaves
3 tablespoons fresh curds
salt to taste

For the seasoning :

½ teaspoon
  mustard seeds
½ teaspoon black
  gram (urad) dal
3 curry leaves
1 small red chilli
a pinch asafoetida (optional)
2 teaspoons oil

1. Put the coconut, gram dal, green chillies, coriander, curry leaves and
2 tablespoons of water in a liquidiser and blend for a few minutes. Do not grind finely.

2. Prepare the seasoning by heating the oil and frying the mustard seeds and
black gram dal seeds until they begin to crackle and then adding the curry leaves,
red chilli and asafoetida.

3. Pour the seasoning over the coconut mixture and add the curds and salt. Mix well.
If the mixture is thick, add a little water.

▶ **Use as required** ◀

GREEN CHUTNEY

Serve with dhoklas and other snacks.

Preparation time : a few minutes. No cooking. Makes 1 cup.

2 teacups chopped coriander
4 green chillies
4 tablespoons grated coconut
1½ teaspoons lemon juice
3 teaspoons sugar
salt to taste

Put all the ingredients in a liquidiser and grind into a paste,
adding a little water if necessary.

▶ **Use as required** ◀

BANANA

And

CUCUMBER SALAD

A kachumbar with a difference.

Preparation time : 10 minutes. No cooking. Serves 6.

3 ripe bananas
3 cucumbers, cut into cubes
2 teaspoons lemon juice
2 green chillies,
finely chopped
3 tablespoons roughly
chopped peanuts

2 tablespoons chopped coriander
2 tablespoons grated fresh
or flaked coconut
1½ teaspoons sugar
salt to taste

1. Peel and cut the bananas into cubes. Mix with the cucumber.
2. Immediately add the lemon juice and mix well.
3. Add the remaining ingredients and chill for 30 minutes.

▶ **Serve cold** ◀

GREEN CHICK PEAS SALAD

Colourful and chat-pati.

Preparation time : 20 minutes. No cooking. Serves 6.

3 teacups boiled
Kabuli chana (chick peas)
1 boiled potato, cut into cubes
1 tomato, chopped
2 tablespoons chopped coriander
2 green chillies,
finely chopped
½ teaspoon black salt
(sanchal)
1 tablespoon lemon juice
2 teaspoons sugar
2 teaspoons chaat masala, page 125.
salt to taste

Clockwise from top: Masala Papad–Page 30,
Sprouted Fruity Bean Salad–Page 29, Mishti Doi–Page 123.

Mix the chick peas with all the ingredients. Chill.

▶ **Serve cold** ◀

SPROUTED FRUITY
BEAN SALAD

Picture on page 27

A typical Indian salad using delicate spices.

Preparation time : 15 minutes. No cooking. Serves 6.

1 orange, segmented
½ teacup raw mango slices (optional)
1 tomato, sliced
1 banana, sliced
1 teacup grapes
½ teacup math sprouts
1 teacup moong sprouts
½ teacup boiled
gram (chana) (optional)
2 tablespoons chopped coriander
1 chopped green chilli
1 teaspoon lemon juice
2 teaspoons sugar
salt to taste

Mix all the ingredients. Chill.

▶ **Serve cold** ◀

Top: Potato Rotis –Page 32 , Bottom: Paneer Koftas in Spinach Sauce –Page 62

MASALA PAPAD

Picture on page 27

Ideal accompaniment for drinks and meals

Preparation time : a few minutes. Cooking time : a few minutes. Serves 6.

6 papads
6 tablespoons finely chopped onions
2 tablespoons finely chopped coriander
½ teaspoon lemon juice or amchur powder
½ teaspoon chilli powder
salt to taste
oil for frying

1. Fry the papad in hot oil.
2. Mix the onions, coriander, lemon juice, chilli powder and salt.
3. Just before serving, sprinkle this mixture on top.

▶ **Serve immediately.** ◀

ROTI, PURI AUR PARATHA

(Indian Breads)

Rotis form a basic part of the *desi* meal. Serving a variety of rotis and parathas in a basket is not only attractive but helps to whet the appetite. In this section, you will find unusual stuffing combinations (like cabbage and paneer, minty corn with vegetables) and unusual methods of preparation. Remember that stuffed rotis or parathas can make a complete meal when served with a bowl of curds or raita.

POTATO ROTIS

Picture on page 28

These soft rotis will melt in your mouth.

Preparation time : 15 minutes. Cooking time : 20 minutes. Makes 4 rotis.

3 potatoes, boiled and mashed
¾ teacup plain flour (maida)
2 tablespoons chopped coriander
3 green chillies, chopped
2 tablespoons melted butter
1 teaspoon salt

For cooking
ghee

1. Sieve the flour.
2. Mix all the ingredients thoroughly and make a soft dough.
Water is not required for this purpose.
3. Divide the dough into 4 portions.
4. Roll out each portion of the dough into a thin round with the help of a little flour.
5. Cook on a hot tawa (griddle) on both sides
using a little ghee until pink spots come on top.

▶ **Serve hot with a curry or dal of your choice** ◀

NOTE : Remember to use old potatoes.

KHAMIRI
GREEN PEAS PURIS

Picture on page 37

Ideal for a rich breakfast.

Preparation time : 20 minutes. Cooking time : 30 minutes. Makes 20 to 25 puris.

For the dough (using yeast)
1½ teacups plain flour (maida)
1½ teacups whole wheat flour
1 teaspoon sugar
2 teaspoons fresh yeast or
1 teaspoon dry yeast
1 tablespoon ghee
1 teaspoon salt

§

**For the dough
(without use of yeast)**
1½ teacups plain flour (maida)
1½ teacups whole wheat flour
1 teaspoon sugar
1 level teaspoon baking powder
3 to 4 tablespoons fresh curds
1 tablespoon ghee
1 teaspoon salt

For the stuffing
2 teacups boiled and mashed green peas
1 teaspoon cumin seeds
2 tablespoons chopped coriander
3 green chillies, chopped
4 teaspoons amchur powder
1 tablespoon ghee
salt to taste

For frying
ghee

For the dough (using yeast)
1. Sieve the flours with the salt.
2. Make a well in the centre. Then add the sugar and ghee and mix well.
3. Crumble the yeast and put in the well.
4. Pour ½ teacup of warm water over the yeast.
Wait for 5 minutes or until bubbles appear on top.
5. Mix the yeast with the flour. Add enough water to make a semi-soft dough.
6. Knead well for 6 minutes and then keep aside for 20 to 30 minutes
or until double in size.

For the dough (without use of yeast)
1. Sieve the flours with the salt.
2. Make a well in the centre. Then add the sugar and ghee and mix well.
3. Add the baking powder and then add the curds on top.
Wait for 1 minute until bubbles appear on top.
4. Make a semi-soft dough by adding enough water.
5. Knead well for 2 minutes and then keep aside for at least 3 to 4 hours.

For the stuffing
1. Heat the ghee and fry the cumin seeds until they begin to crackle.
2. Add the remaining ingredients and mix well.

How to proceed

1. Knead the dough and divide into 8 portions.
2. Roll out each portion of the dough into a small thick round.
3. Spread a little stuffing on one round, fold the edges towards the centre and close. Roll out again.
4. Repeat for the remaining rounds and stuffing.
5. Wait for 10 to 15 minutes.
6. Fry the puris with a little ghee in a shallow frying pan. Press and fry on one side, and then repeat for the other side.

▶ *Serve hot* ◀

PARATHAS STUFFED
With
VEGETABLES AND CHEESE

Picture on page 38

Cook these tasty parathas in front of your guests. They make a meal by themselves with a bowl of curds.

Preparation time : 20 minutes. Cooking time : 20 minutes. Makes 10 parathas.

For the dough
1½ teacups plain flour (maida)
1½ teacups whole wheat flour
1 tablespoon ghee
¾ teaspoon salt

§

To be ground into a paste (for the stuffing)
3 green chillies
2 tablespoons chopped coriander
25 mm. piece ginger

For the stuffing
3 carrots, finely chopped
1 small cauliflower, finely chopped
2 potatoes, finely chopped
1 teacup green peas
1 teaspoon cumin seeds
4 tablespoons grated cheese
2 green chillies, chopped
2 tablespoons chopped coriander
2 tablespoons ghee
salt to taste

For cooking
ghee

For the dough
1. Sieve the flours with the salt.
2. Add the ghee and mix well. Add enough water and make a semi-soft dough.

For the stuffing
1. Heat the ghee and fry the cumin seeds until they begin to crackle.
2. Add the chopped vegetables, green peas, paste and 2 to 3 tablespoons of water and cook on a slow flame until the vegetables become soft.
Alternatively, cook in a pressure cooker without adding any water.
3. Mash the vegetables slightly, add the cheese, green chillies, coriander and salt and mix well.

How to proceed
1. Knead the dough and divide into 20 portions.
2. Roll out each portion of the dough into a small thin round with the help of flour.
3. Spread a little filling on one round, cover with the other round and press well.
4. Cook on a hot tawa (griddle) on both sides using a little ghee until pink spots come on top.
5. Repeat for the remaining rounds and stuffing.

▶ *Serve hot* ◀

PANEER

And

SPINACH PARATHAS

Picture on page 38

They look delicious and taste delicious.

Preparation time : 20 minutes. Cooking time : 15 minutes. Makes 6 parathas.

For the dough

1½ teacups plain flour (maida)
1½ teacups whole wheat flour
2 teacups chopped spinach
½ teaspoon lemon juice
2 tablespoons ghee
1 teaspoon salt

§

To be mixed into a stuffing

1 teacup grated cauliflower
1 teacup crumbled paneer, page 126
2 tablespoons chopped coriander
3 to 4 green chillies, chopped
½ teaspoon finely chopped ginger
salt to taste

For cooking

ghee

For the dough

1. Blend the spinach and lemon juice with 2 tablespoons of water in a liquidiser.
2. Sieve the flours with the salt. Add the ghee and mix well.
3. Add the spinach mixture. Make a semi-soft dough by adding enough water.

How to proceed

1. Divide the dough into 6 portions.
2. Roll out one portion of the dough, put about 2 teaspoons of the stuffing
in the centre and seal the edges.
3. Roll out again into a thick paratha.
4. Cook on a hot tawa (griddle) on both sides using a little ghee
until pink spots come on top.
5. Repeat for the remaining dough portions and stuffing.

▶ *Serve hot with fresh curds* ◀

ONION ROTIS

Pop these rotis in a toaster just before eating and serve with butter.

Preparation time : 20 minutes. Cooking time : 30 minutes. Makes 6 rotis.

1½ teacups whole wheat flour
2 onions, chopped
2 tablespoons chopped coriander
2 to 3 green chillies, chopped

1 teaspoon cumin seeds
½ teaspoon grated ginger
2 tablespoons melted ghee
¾ teaspoon salt

For cooking

ghee

Anti-clockwise from top : Corn Curry – Page 50
Moghlai Aloo – Page 47, *Khamiri Green Peas Puris –* Page 32

1. Sieve the flour with the salt.
2. Mix all the ingredients thoroughly and make a stiff dough by adding just enough water.
3. Knead the dough and divide the dough into 6 portions.
4. Roll out each portion of the dough into a thick round of about 150 mm. diameter with the help of flour.
5. Make a few light, horizontal slits on one side of each round.
6. Cook on a hot tawa (griddle) on both sides using a little ghee until pink spots come on top.

▶ Serve hot ◀

ɷ

SPICY URAD DAL PURIS

Picture on page 66

A spicy and tasty version of a popular puri.

Preparation time : 20 minutes. Cooking time : 30 minutes. Makes 10 puris.

For the dough
2 teacups plain flour (maida)
2 tablespoons hot oil
½ teaspoon nigella (kalonji) seeds
2 pinches salt

For the masala powder (for the stuffing)
1 tablespoon coriander seeds
1 tablespoon cumin seeds
1 teaspoon aniseed (saunf)
8 black peppercorns
4 large or 8 small red chillies

For the stuffing
¾ teacup black gram (urad) dal
2 tablespoons oil
salt to taste

For deep frying
oil or ghee

For the dough
1. Mix all the ingredients and add enough water to make a stiff dough.
2. Knead well and keep aside for 20 minutes.

In Paratha Basket: *Parathas Stuffed with Vegetables and Cheese (Square)* – *Page 34* ,
Paneer and Spinach Parathas (Green) – *Page 35* , *Cabbage and Paneer Parathas (Round)* – *Page 42*   39

For the masala powder (for the stuffing)

1. Roast the ingredients on a hot tawa (griddle) without any fat for 1 minute. Cool.
2. Grind into a powder.

For the stuffing

1. Soak the urad dal in water for 4 hours. Drain.
2. Grind coarsely in a grinder using very little water.
3. Heat the oil and fry the dal paste until light golden in colour. Cool.
4. Add the masala powder and salt. Mix well.

How to proceed

1. Knead the dough and divide into 10 portions.
2. Roll out each portion of the dough into a thin round of about 50 mm. diameter with the help of flour.
3. Put a little stuffing mixture in each round. Close the edges to cover the stuffing completely and roll out again into small puris.
4. Deep fry the puris in hot oil until golden brown.

▶ **Serve hot with fresh curds** ◀

CORIANDER ROTIS

Picture on page 55

Coriander lends a delicious flavour to these rotis. Ideal for breakfast.

Preparation time : 20 minutes. Cooking time : 30 minutes. Makes 8 rotis.

For the dough

1½ teacups whole wheat flour
4 teaspoons oil
½ teaspoon salt

To be mixed into a stuffing

1 teacup chopped coriander
2 teaspoons coriander-cumin seed (dhana-jira) powder
¼ level teaspoon turmeric powder
1 tablespoon gram flour (besan)
3 green chillies, finely chopped
salt to taste

Other ingredients

oil for brushing

For the dough

1. Mix all the ingredients and add enough water to make a semi-stiff dough.
2. Knead well and divide into 8 equal portions.
3. Roll out each portion into a thick round
   with the help of flour.

How to proceed

1. Divide the stuffing into 8 equal portions.
2. Brush each dough round with a little oil and spread one stuffing portion on it.
3. Roll out into a cigar shape.
4. Make a small round like a coil and press lightly by hand.
5. Roll out again into a thick roti.
6. Repeat for the remaining dough and stuffing.
7. Cook on a hot tawa (griddle) on both sides
   until pink spots come on top.

➤ *Spread ghee or butter on top and serve hot* ◀

MINTY CORN

And

VEGETABLE PARATHAS

A minty cover with a spicy filling.

Preparation time : 20 minutes. Cooking time : 40 minutes. Makes 15 parathas.

For the dough

1½ teacups plain flour (maida)
1½ teacups whole wheat flour
1 tablespoon melted ghee

To be blended into a mint sauce (for the dough)

2 tablespoons mint leaves
1 teaspoon lemon juice
½ teaspoon cumin seeds
½ teacup water
3 green chillies
1 teaspoon salt

For the stuffing

½ teacup finely chopped cabbage
1¼ teacups fresh or
frozen corn, cooked
2 potatoes, peeled and chopped
1 onion, chopped
juice of 1 lemon

½ teaspoon garam masala, page 125
1 tablespoon chopped coriander
1 teaspoon ground green chilli
1 teaspoon sugar
1 tablespoon oil
salt to taste

For cooking
ghee

For the dough
1. Mix the flours, ghee and the mint sauce and make a soft dough,
adding water if necessary.
2. Knead well and divide into 15 portions.
3. Roll out each portion into a very thin round of about 150 mm. diameter.
4. Cook lightly on a hot tawa (griddle) on both sides without using ghee.

For the stuffing
1. Sprinkle salt over the cabbage and keep aside.
After 10 minutes, squeeze out the water.
2. Crush the cooked corn.
3. Heat the oil and add the potatoes, sprinkle a little water, cover and cook until soft.
4. Add the cabbage and onion and cook for 1 minute.
5. Add the corn, lemon juice, garam masala, coriander, green chilli,
sugar and salt and cook for 1 minute.

How to proceed
1. Put 2 tablespoons of the stuffing in the centre of each dough round.
2. Fold towards the centre from all 4 sides and press to seal.
3. Repeat for the remaining rounds and stuffing.
4. Brush lightly with ghee and cook on a hot tawa (griddle)
on both sides using a little ghee until pink spots come on top

▶ *Serve hot* ◀

CABBAGE

And

PANEER PARATHAS

Picture on page 38

You will enjoy these parathas with a novel filling.

Preparation time : 15 minutes. Cooking time : 30 minutes. Makes 5 parathas.

For the dough
1½ teacups whole wheat flour or
plain flour (maida)
½ teaspoon salt
1 tablespoon melted ghee

For the stuffing
1½ teacups grated cabbage
¾ teacup crumbled paneer, page 126
2 tablespoons chopped coriander
2 green chillies, finely chopped
salt to taste

For cooking
ghee

For the dough
1. Sieve the flour with the salt.
2. Add the ghee and mix well.
3. Add enough water to make a soft dough.
4. Knead well for 3 to 4 minutes.

For the stuffing
1. Sprinkle salt over the cabbage and keep aside.
After 10 minutes, squeeze out the water
2. Add the paneer, coriander, green chillies and salt and mix well.

How to proceed
1. Divide the dough into 10 portions.
2. Roll out each portion of the dough into a round of about 100 mm. diameter
with help of flour.
3. Spread a little stuffing on one round and cover with another round.
Press the sides well.
4. Cook on a hot tawa (griddle) on both sides using a little ghee
until pink spots come on top.

▶ **Serve hot** ◀

SPICY PARATHAS

Try these parathas with a rich masala filling.

Preparation time : 20 minutes. Cooking time : 30 minutes. Makes 12 parathas.

For the dough
2½ teacups whole wheat flour
2 tablespoons melted ghee
½ teaspoon salt

**For the masala
(for the stuffing)**

2 teaspoons cumin seeds
¼ teaspoon asafoetida
4 red chillies
4 cardamoms
4 cloves
2 sticks cinnamon

For the stuffing

4 tablespoons poppy seeds
(khus-khus)
½ teaspoon nigella
seeds (kalonji)
½ teaspoon ground ginger
2 teaspoons ghee
salt to taste

For cooking
ghee

For the parathas
1. Sieve the flour with the salt.
2. Add the ghee and mix well.
3. Add enough water to make a soft dough.
4. Knead well and keep aside for 30 minutes.

For the masala (for the stuffing)
1. Roast the ingredients on a hot tawa (griddle) without any fat for 1 minute. Cool.
2. Grind into a powder.

For the stuffing
1. Soak the poppy seeds in a small quantity of water for 2 hours.
2. Grind the soaked seeds to a paste with a little water.
3. Heat the ghee and fry the nigella seeds and ginger for a few seconds.
4. Add the poppy seed paste and cook for 1 minute.
5. Remove from the heat.
6. Add the ground masala and salt and mix.

How to proceed
1. Knead the dough and divide into 12 portions.
2. Roll out each portion of the dough into a round of about 75 mm. diameter with the help of flour.
3. Spread 1 teaspoon of the stuffing evenly over each round.
Fold the rounds in half and again spread over a little stuffing over each.
Then again fold into a quarter round.
4. Seal the edges with a little paste made of flour and water.
5. On a lightly floured surface, roll out into triangular parathas.
6. Cook on a hot tawa (griddle) on both sides using a little ghee until pink spots come on top.

 Serve hot ◄

DESI TARKARIYAN

(Vegetable Dishes)

A variety of gravies has been used for the vegetable
dishes in this section. For example, a red gravy
is used for Baked Paneer Mutter and for Moghlai
Aloo. In contrast, a green gravy (made from fresh
coriander/spinach leaves) is used in Corn Curry
and in Paneer Koftas in Spinach Sauce. And in
dishes like Malbari Curry and Ceylonese Curry,
the South Indian style of gravies and curries using
coconut milk is used.

VEGETABLE CURRY
In TOMATO SAUCE

This curry can be served both as a dal and as a sabzi.

Preparation time : 20 minutes. Cooking time : 25 minutes. Serves 8.

1 ½ kg. tomatoes,
cut into big pieces
2 potatoes
10 to 12 guar
10 to 12 ladies fingers (bhindi)
10 to 12 french beans
2 drumsticks
1 teaspoon mustard seeds

1 teaspoon cumin seeds
2 pinches asafoetida
3 tablespoons gram flour (besan)
a few curry leaves
a few slit green chillies
2 pinches garam masala, page 125
3 tablespoons ghee
salt to taste

To be ground into a paste

10 green chillies
25 mm. piece ginger

1. Add 4 teacups of water to the tomatoes and cook for 10 minutes.
2. When cooked, take out a thick purée by passing through a sieve.
3. Cut the potatoes and the vegetables into big pieces.
4. Heat the ghee and fry the mustard seeds and cumin seeds until they begin to crackle.
5. Add the asafoetida and the gram flour and cook on a slow flame
for at least 2 to 3 minutes.
6. Add the tomato purée, vegetables, curry leaves, green chillies, garam masala,
paste and salt and cook for 15 to 20 minutes or until the vegetable are soft.

▶ **Serve hot** ◀

CEYLONESE CURRY

Picture on page 56

A sure hit at any party.

Preparation time : 30 minutes. Cooking time : 15 minutes. Serves 4.

For the Ceylonese curry

2 large coconuts
1 teacup chopped mixed vegetables
(french beans, carrots, green peas)
1/4 teaspoon turmeric powder
3 teaspoons coriander-cumin seed
(dhana-jira) powder
2 teaspoons chilli powder
2 onions, chopped
4 curry leaves
2 slit green chillies

5 peppercorns
3 small sticks cinnamon
1/2 teaspoon fenugreek
(methi) seeds
2 boiled potatoes,
finely chopped
3 large tomatoes,
finely chopped
salt to taste

To be ground into Sambol chutney

1/2 coconut, grated
1 onion, chopped
1 teaspoon chilli powder
1 teaspoon lemon juice
salt to taste

To serve

2 to 3 teacups boiled rice or noodles

1. Grate the coconut. Add 5 1/2 teacups of water and blend in a liquidiser.
Strain and take out the coconut milk. Keep aside.
2. To the coconut milk, add the vegetables, turmeric powder,
coriander-cumin seed powder, chilli powder, onions, curry leaves,
green chillies, peppercorns, cinnamon, fenugreek seeds and salt.
3. Cook until the vegetables are tender. Add the potatoes and tomatoes
and boil for a few minutes more.

▶ *Serve hot with Sambol chutney and boiled rice or noodles* ◀

MOGHLAI ALOO

Picture on page 37

A ever-popular aloo sabzi.

Preparation time : 15 minutes. Cooking time : 20 minutes. Serves 4.

10 to 12 small potatoes
3/4 teacup fresh curds
2 onions, grated
2 teaspoons coriander-cumin seed
(dhana-jira) powder
1 teaspoon chilli powder

1/4 teaspoon turmeric powder
1 teacup boiled green peas
2 tablespoons fresh cream
1/2 teaspoon sugar
3 tablespoons ghee
salt to taste

To be ground into a paste
3 cloves garlic
4 cloves
2 to 3 tablespoons poppy seeds (khus-khus)
12 mm. piece ginger
2 green chillies
2 cardamoms

1. Peel the potatoes. Prick them thoroughly with a toothpick and soak in cold water. After about 10 minutes, remove from the water and add the curds and salt. Keep aside for 1 hour.
2. Heat the ghee and fry the onions for 1 minute. Add the paste and fry again for 1 minute.
3. Add the coriander-cumin seed powder, chilli powder and turmeric powder and fry again for a few seconds.
4. Add the potato mixture and 2 teacups of water. Cover and cook until the potatoes are soft.
5. Add the green peas, cream and sugar.

▶ **Serve hot** ◀

Note : If you like, you can fry the potatoes in ghee and omit the soaking stage in step 1.

GREEN PEAS AMBTI

A spicy Maharashtrian vegetable.

Preparation time : 20 minutes. Cooking time : 25 minutes. Serves 6.

4 teacups green peas
4 large tomatoes
3 tablespoons oil
salt to taste

For the paste

1 onion, chopped
2 tablespoons grated coconut
3 teaspoons coriander seeds
3 sticks cinnamon
1 teaspoon cumin seeds

3 cloves
3 black peppercorns
6 red chillies
6 cloves garlic
1 tablespoon oil

To serve

2 tablespoons fresh cream
2 tablespoons chopped coriander

For the paste

1. Heat the oil and fry the onion, coconut, coriander seeds, cinnamon, cumin seeds, cloves, peppercorns and chillies for at least 3 to 4 minutes.
2. Grind the fried ingredients with the garlic to make a paste.

For the ambti

1. Crush the green peas.
2. Put the tomatoes in hot water for 10 minutes. Grate into a purée.
3. Heat the oil and fry the paste for a few minutes.
4. Add the green peas, tomato purée, salt and 1½ teacups of water and bring to boil. Reduce the heat and simmer for about 15 minutes.

▶ *Serve hot topped with the cream and coriander* ◀

SPICY CORN

With

GREEN PEAS

Corn and green peas enlivened by rich spices.

Preparation time : 15 minutes. Cooking time : 25 minutes. Serves 4.

2 teacups boiled corn	**To be ground into a paste**
1 teacup boiled green peas	5 cloves garlic
2 large tomatoes	2 large onions
1 teacup milk	10 red chillies
½ teacup fresh curds	2 teaspoons coriander seeds
2 tablespoons ground poppy seeds	1 teaspoon cumin seeds
(khus-khus)	2 sticks cinnamon
½ teaspoon sugar	2 cloves
3 tablespoons ghee	25 mm. piece ginger
salt to taste	

1. Put the tomatoes in hot water for 10 minutes. Grate into a purée.
2. Heat the ghee and fry the paste for 3 to 4 minutes. Add the tomato purée and fry again for a while.
3. Add the green peas, corn and 1½ teacups of water and cook for a few minutes.
4. Mix the milk, curds and poppy seeds and add to the vegetables. Add the sugar and salt and boil for 5 minutes.

▶ **Serve hot** ◀

CORN CURRY

Picture on page 37

Coconut and coriander add subtlety to this delicious green curry.

Preparation time : 15 minutes. Cooking time : 10 minutes. Serves 4.

2 teacups cooked corn
1 fresh coconut
2 sticks cinnamon
2 cloves
2 cardamoms
juice of ½ lemon
2 tablespoons ghee
salt to taste

To be ground into a paste

1 onion
1 teacup chopped coriander
6 green chillies
1 tablespoon grated fresh coconut
7 cloves garlic
4 teaspoons poppy seeds (khus-khus)
25 mm. piece ginger

1. Grate the coconut. Add 4 teacups of water and blend in a liquidiser. Strain and take out coconut milk.
2. Heat the ghee and fry the paste for 2 minutes.
3. Add the cinnamon, cloves and cardamoms and fry again for a while.
4. Add the lemon juice and mix well.
5. Add the corn, coconut milk and salt, mix well and cook for a few minutes.

▶ **Serve hot** ◀

MASALA CORN

Corn vegetable with a difference.

Preparation time : 20 minutes. Cooking time : 25 minutes. Serves 4.

300 grams cooked sweet corn
8 to 10 small onions
10 to 12 small new potatoes
1 onion, chopped
1 capsicum, chopped
1 tomato, chopped
1 teaspoon chilli powder

3 green chillies, chopped
3 teaspoons vinegar
3 tablespoons oil
salt to taste
ghee for deep frying
chopped spring onions to garnish

To be ground into a chilli-ginger paste

4 green chillies
1 onion, chopped
12 mm. piece ginger

1. Boil the whole onions in salted water until tender.
2. Heat the ghee and deep fry the potatoes until golden.
3. Heat the oil and fry the chopped onion for a few minutes.
4. Add the paste and fry for a few more minutes.
5. Add the capsicum, tomato and chilli powder and fry for at least 3 to 4 minutes.
6. Add the corn, cooked onions, potatoes, green chillies, vinegar and salt and cook for a few minutes, stirring occasionally.
7. Sprinkle spring onions on top.

▶ *Serve immediately* ◀

CAULIFLOWER CURRY

An everyday vegetable.

Preparation time : 15 minutes. Cooking time : 30 minutes. Serves 4.

3 large tomatoes	**To be ground into a paste**
4 onions, finely chopped	5 green chillies
1 kg. cauliflower, grated	6 to 7 cloves garlic
¼ teaspoon turmeric powder	25 mm. piece ginger
100 grams crumbled paneer, page 126	3 cloves
5 to 6 tablespoons oil	3 cardamoms
salt to taste	8 to 10 peppercorns
1 tablespoon chopped	1 teaspoon cumin seeds
coriander for garnishing	1½ teaspoons chilli powder

1. Put the tomatoes in hot water for 10 minutes. Grate into a purée.
2. Heat the oil and fry the onions till golden in colour.
   Add the paste and fry again for 3 to 4 minutes.
3. Add the cauliflower, turmeric powder and ½ teacup of water.
   Cover and cook for 10 to 12 minutes.
4. Remove the cover and go on stirring for 2 to 3 minutes.
5. Add the paneer and mix well.
6. Add the tomato purée and salt and cook until the oil floats on top.
7. Sprinkle the coriander on top.

▶ *Serve hot with parathas* ◀

BREAD KOFTAS
In
PUMPKIN CURRY

Mouth-melting bread koftas in delicious pumpkin curry.

Preparation time : 25 minutes. Cooking time : 30 minutes. Serves 4.

For the koftas
5 to 6 bread slices
½ teacup fresh curds
3 level tablespoons
plain flour (maida)
1 tablespoon chopped coriander
4 green chillies, chopped
2 pinches soda bi-carb
salt to taste
oil for deep frying

For the pumpkin curry
250 grams white pumpkin (lauki)
2 large tomatoes
3 onions, grated
2 teaspoons chilli powder
1 tablespoon coriander-cumin
seed (dhana-jira) powder
¼ teaspoon turmeric powder
1 teaspoon garam masala, page 125
1 teacup fresh curds
½ teacup boiled green peas
1 teacup boiled and
fried small potatoes
3 tablespoons ghee
salt to taste

For the koftas
1. Remove the crust from the bread slices.
2. Soak the bread in the curds for 20 minutes.
3. Add the flour, coriander, chillies, soda bi-carb and salt and mix thoroughly.
4. Divide and shape into balls.
5. Deep fry in oil.

For the pumpkin curry
1. Peel the pumpkin and cut into big pieces.
2. Add 1½ teacups of water and cook. When cooked, blend in a liquidiser.
3. Put the tomatoes in hot water for 10 minutes. Grate into a purée.
4. Heat the ghee and fry the onions until light brown in colour.
5. Add the chilli powder, coriander-cumin seed powder,
turmeric powder and garam masala and fry for a few seconds.
6. Add the curds, pumpkin gravy, tomato purée, ½ teacup of water
and cook for a few minutes.
7. Add the green peas, potatoes and salt.

How to serve
When ready to serve, add the koftas to the curry and give one boil.

▶ *Serve immediately* ◀

BAKED PANEER MUTTER

The popular Indian dish cooked in a Western manner.

Preparation time : 20 minutes. Cooking time : 30 minutes. Serves 4.

For the paneer mixture
225 grams paneer, page 126
2 green chillies,
finely chopped
salt to taste

For the green peas mixture
450 grams green peas
3 tomatoes, cut into big pieces
1 tablespoon fresh cream
1/2 teaspoon sugar
2 tablespoons ghee
salt to taste

To be ground into a paste (for the green peas mixture)
6 cloves garlic
25 mm. piece ginger
8 red chillies
1 tablespoon chopped cashewnuts
1 tablespoon poppy seeds (khus-khus)
2 teaspoons coriander seeds
1 teaspoon cumin seeds

For the white sauce
1 level tablespoon plain flour (maida)
1 teacup milk
1 tablespoon butter

For the paneer mixture
1. Cut the paneer into cubes.
2. Mix the green chillies and salt with the paneer cubes very well.

For the green peas mixture
1. Add 1 tablespoon of water to the tomatoes and cook until soft.
Blend in a liquidiser and take out a thick purée.
2. Heat the ghee and fry the paste for 2 to 3 minutes.
Add the tomato purée and green peas and cook for a few minutes.
3. Add the cream, sugar and salt.

For the white sauce
1. Melt the butter.
2. Add the flour and cook on a slow flame while stirring throughout, until froth appears.
3. Gradually, add the milk and stir continually until the sauce thickens.

How to proceed

1. Mix the paneer mixture with the white sauce.
2. Spread the green peas mixture in a greased baking dish.
3. Spread the paneer mixture over it and bake in a hot oven at 230°C (450°F) for 20 minutes.

▶ *Serve immediately* ◀

SPICY KOFTA CURRY

Spicy and tasty.

Preparation time : 15 minutes. Cooking time : 20 minutes. Serves 4.

For the koftas

¾ teacup fresh curds
¾ teacup gram flour (besan)
2 tablespoons chopped coriander
6 green chillies, chopped
1 teaspoon cumin seeds
2 pinches soda bi-carb
salt to taste
oil or ghee for deep frying

For the curry

2 large tomatoes
½ teacup milk
2 tablespoons fresh cream
½ teaspoon sugar
3 tablespoons ghee
salt to taste

To be ground into a paste (for the curry)

1 onion
4 cloves garlic
2 teaspoons coriander seeds
1 teaspoon cumin seeds
2 teaspoons poppy seeds (khus-khus)
25 mm. piece ginger
2 green chillies
6 red chillies
1 tablespoon chopped coriander
¼ teaspoon turmeric powder

For the koftas

1. Mix all the ingredients to make a thick batter.
2. Heat the oil, drop spoonfuls of the batter into it and deep fry until golden brown. Repeat for the remaining batter.

Anti-clockwise from top: Coriander Rotis–Page 40,
Paneer Makhani–Page 57, Mixed Vegetables – Patiala Style–Page 61

For the curry

1. Cut the tomatoes into big pieces, add 1 teacup of water and cook. When cooked, take out a purée by passing through a sieve.
2. Heat the ghee and fry the paste for 3 to 4 minutes.
3. Add the tomato purée, milk and ½ teacup of water and boil for 10 minutes.
4. Add the cream, sugar, salt and koftas and give one boil.

▶ *Serve immediately with rice or parathas* ◀

PANEER MAKHANI

Picture on page 55

A popular vegetable from the Punjab.

Preparation time : 15 minutes. Cooking time : 25 minutes. Serves 4.

250 grams paneer, page 126
2 tablespoons fresh curds
3 large tomatoes
3 onions, grated
1 teaspoon garam masala, page 125
2 teaspoons coriander-cumin seed (dhana-jira) powder
1½ teaspoons chilli powder

¼ teaspoon turmeric powder
100 grams fresh cream
2 teaspoons butter
4 tablespoons ghee
salt to taste
ghee for deep frying
chopped coriander for garnishing

1. Cut the paneer in the shape of fingers and deep fry lightly in ghee.
2. Apply the curds to the fried paneer.
3. Put the tomatoes in hot water for 5 minutes. Take out the skin and chop finely.
4. Heat the ghee and fry the onions until light pink in colour.
5. Add the garam masala, coriander-cumin seed powder, chilli powder, turmeric powder and salt and fry for 1 minute.
6. Add the tomatoes and fry for at least 5 minutes or until ghee floats on top.
7. Add 1 teacup of water and the cream. Cook for a few minutes and then add the butter.
8. Add the paneer and cook for a while. Garnish with coriander.

▶ *Serve hot with naan* ◀

MIXED VEGETABLES – BHOPALI STYLE

You are sure to enjoy this creamy vegetable.

Preparation time : 20 minutes. Cooking time : 20 minutes. Serves 6.

2½ teacups mixed boiled
vegetables (potatoes, carrots,
french beans, cauliflower,
green peas)
2 tablespoons cashewnuts
3 tablespoons milk
2 tablespoons fresh cream
2 pinches sugar
5 tablespoons oil or ghee
salt to taste

To be ground into a paste
8 to 10 cloves garlic
10 green chillies
6 tablespoons chopped coriander
6 cloves
4 cardamoms
1 tablespoon coriander seeds
2 teaspoons cumin seeds
25 mm. piece ginger

1. Heat the oil and fry the cashewnuts. Remove from the pan and keep aside.
2. Fry the paste in the same oil for 2 to 3 minutes.
3. Add the vegetables and fry for 1 minute.
Add ¾ teacup of water and cook until the vegetables are soft.
4. Mix the milk and cream and add to the vegetables. Add the sugar and salt.

▶ **Top with the fried cashewnuts and serve hot** ◀

STUFFED TOMATOES

Cabbage makes an excellent stuffing for tomatoes.

Preparation time : 20 minutes. Cooking time : 10 minutes. Serves 6.

¾ kg. tomatoes
1 cabbage (450 grams approx.),
grated
½ teaspoon turmeric powder
2 teaspoons coriander-cumin seed
(dhana-jira) powder

2 teaspoons chilli powder
2 teaspoons sugar
4 tablespoons
chopped coriander
salt to taste

58

1. Sprinkle about 1 teaspoon of salt over the cabbage and keep aside for 10 minutes. Squeeze out the water.
2. Add the turmeric powder, coriander-cumin seed powder, chilli powder, sugar and salt.
3. Add the chopped coriander, keeping aside a little for garnish.
4. Make four slits in each tomato and stuff with the cabbage mixture.
5. Cover and cook for 10 minutes until the tomatoes are soft.

▶ *Garnish with the balance chopped coriander and serve hot* ◀

STUFFED POTATOES

And
TOMATOES

The rich stuffing transforms the lowly potatoes and tomatoes.

Preparation time : 20 minutes. Cooking time : 20 minutes. Serves 6 to 8.

15 potatoes	**For the paste**
10 tomatoes	1 onion, sliced
6 teaspoons oil	½ dried coconut, grated
a pinch asafoetida	10 cloves garlic
3 tablespoons	3 tablespoons coriander seeds
chopped coriander	3 tablespoons aniseed (saunf)
	2 tablespoons poppy seeds
	(khus-khus)
	10 black peppercorns
	2 teaspoons chilli powder
	1 teaspoon turmeric powder
	4 tablespoons chopped coriander
	2 tablespoons oil
	salt to taste

For the paste
1. Heat the oil and gently fry the onion, coconut, garlic, coriander seeds, aniseed, poppy seeds and peppercorns for 2 minutes.
2. Blend the mixture into a paste in a blender with a little water.
3. Add the chilli and turmeric powders, coriander and salt.

How to proceed

1. Make four slits in each potato and tomato and stuff with the paste.
2. Heat the oil and add the stuffed potatoes and tomatoes,
the asafoetida and 4 teacups of water.
Cover and cook over medium heat for 20 minutes or until the vegetables are soft.

▶ *Sprinkle coriander on top and serve hot* ◀

MALBARI CURRY

Picture on page 93

Coconut gives the dish its distinctive aroma.

Preparation time : 20 minutes. Cooking time : 25 minutes. Serves 6.

½ coconut, grated	**For the paste**
2½ teacups mixed boiled	½ coconut, grated or
vegetables (french beans, carrots,	25 grams desiccated coconut
potatoes, cauliflower, green peas)	3 to 4 curry leaves
1 onion, chopped	1 tablespoon cooked rice
2 curry leaves	2 green chillies
¼ teaspoon turmeric powder	6 cloves garlic
1 tomato, chopped	1 stick cinnamon
½ teaspoon lemon juice	3 cloves
salt to taste	4 black peppercorns
	3 red chillies

For the paste

1. Mix the coconut, curry leaves and rice and cook on a slow flame,
stirring continuously, until the mixture is light pink.
2. Add the green chillies, garlic, cinnamon, cloves, peppercorns and red chillies
and blend with a little water.

How to proceed

1. Add 2 teacups of water to the grated coconut and blend in a liquidiser.
Strain and take out the coconut milk.
2. Add the paste, all the vegetables (except the tomato), onion, curry leaves and
turmeric powder and cook for 15 to 20 minutes or until the vegetables are soft.
3. Add the the chopped tomato and cook for 2 to 3 minutes.
4. Add the lemon juice and salt.

▶ **Serve hot** ◀

MIXED VEGETABLES – PATIALA STYLE

Picture on page 55

A delicately spiced vegetable.

Preparation time : 10 minutes. Cooking time : 20 minutes. Serves 6.

2½ teacups mixed boiled vegetables
(cauliflower, carrots, green peas)
2 to 3 tablespoons chopped capsicum
1 onion, finely chopped
¼ teaspoon turmeric powder
1 green chilli, finely chopped

1 teacup milk
½ teaspoon sugar
½ teaspoon cinnamon powder
1 level teaspoon cornflour
1 tablespoon chopped coriander
3 tablespoons ghee
salt to taste

To be ground into a paste
3 cloves garlic
12 mm. piece ginger

1. Heat the ghee and fry the onion for 1 minute.
2. Mix the paste in 2 tablespoons of water and add along with the turmeric powder. Cook until the onions are soft.
4. Add the boiled vegetables, capsicum, green chilli, milk, sugar, cinnamon powder and salt.
5. Mix the cornflour with 3 tablespoons of water and add to the mixture. Cook for 2 to 3 minutes.

▶ **Sprinkle coriander on top and serve hot** ◀

PUMPKIN
And
POTATOES – RAJASTHANI STYLE

Picture on page 66

Serve this Marwari sabzi with urad dal puris.

Preparation time : 15 minutes. Cooking time : 15 minutes. Serves 6 to 8.

450 grams red pumpkin (kaddu),
    chopped
450 grams potatoes, chopped
2 bay leaves
12 mm. stick cinnamon
2 cloves
2 cardamoms
1 teaspoon nigella seeds (kalonji)
½ teaspoon mustard seeds
½ teaspoon fenugreek
    (methi) seeds
2 tablespoons fresh curds

¼ teaspoon asafoetida
1 teaspoon chilli powder
2 teaspoons coriander-cumin seed
    (dhana-jira) powder
½ teaspoon turmeric powder
1 tomato, chopped
1 teaspoon amchur powder
    or lemon juice
½ teaspoon sugar
3 tablespoons ghee
salt to taste

1. Heat the ghee and fry the bay leaves, cinnamon, cloves, cardamoms, nigella seeds, mustard seeds and fenugreek seeds until the seeds begin to crackle.
2. Add the curds, asafoetida, chilli, coriander-cumin seed and turmeric powders and fry for 2 to 3 minutes.
3. Add the tomato and fry for 1 minute.
4. Add the potatoes, pumpkin and ½ teacup of water, cover and cook on a medium heat for 10 to 12 minutes or until the vegetables are tender.
5. Add the amchur powder, sugar and salt.

▶ **Serve hot** ◀

PANEER KOFTAS

In

SPINACH SAUCE

Picture on page 28

Soft delicious koftas in rich spinach gravy.

Preparation time : 15 minutes. Cooking time : 30 minutes. Serves 6.

For the spinach sauce
2 teacups finely chopped spinach
¾ teacup fresh curds
½ teaspoon sugar
2 tablespoons ghee
salt to taste

To be ground into a paste (for the spinach sauce)

1 tablespoon grated coconut
1 tablespoon chopped cashewnuts
1 tablespoon poppy seeds
(khus-khus)
4 cloves garlic
4 to 5 green chillies
25 mm. piece ginger
1 teaspoon aniseed (saunf)

For the koftas

175 grams paneer, page 126
4 level tablespoons plain flour
(maida)
2 tablespoons chopped coriander
2 green chillies,
finely chopped
a pinch soda bi-carb
salt to taste
oil for deep frying

For the spinach sauce

1. Cook the spinach with ½ teacup of water.
2. When cooked, blend in a liquidiser.
3. Heat the ghee and fry the paste for 3 to 4 minutes.
4. Add the curds and fry again for 1 minute.
5. Add the spinach purée, sugar and salt and boil for 3 to 4 minutes.

For the koftas

1. Mix all the ingredients except the oil and shape into small balls.
2. Deep fry in hot oil until golden brown.

How to serve

Just before serving, add the koftas to the spinach sauce and bring to the boil.

▶ *Serve hot* ◀

GREEN PEAS

And

MUSHROOM CURRY

A curry for the mushroom lovers.

Preparation time : 15 minutes. Cooking time : 15 minutes. Serves 6.

1 teacup green peas, boiled
1 small can (400 grams) mushrooms,
drained and sliced
1 onion, chopped
2 cloves garlic, chopped

1 tablespoon raisins
3 tablespoons fresh cream
4 tablespoons fresh curds
2 tablespoons ghee
salt to taste

To be ground into a paste

5 cloves	2 tablespoons poppy seeds
25 mm. piece ginger	(khus-khus)
2 tablespoons chopped	2 cardamoms
cashewnuts	4 green chillies

1. Heat the ghee and fry the onion until golden.
2. Add the garlic and fry for 30 seconds.
3. Add the paste and fry for 2 to 3 minutes.
4. Add the green peas, mushrooms, raisins, cream, curds, ½ teacup of water and salt and cook for 5 minutes.

▶ **Serve hot** ◀

QUICK POTATO CURRY

Children's favourite.

Preparation time : 10 minutes. Cooking time : 10 minutes. Serves 4.

For the tomato paste

2 tomatoes
1 onion, finely chopped
1 teaspoon finely chopped ginger
1 teaspoon finely chopped garlic
1 teaspoon chilli powder

Other ingredients

10 to 12 small potatoes, boiled and peeled
2 sticks cinnamon
2 cloves
2 cardamoms
4 tablespoons fresh cream
½ teaspoon sugar (optional)
salt to taste
2 tablespoons butter

For the tomato paste

Blend the tomatoes, onion, ginger, garlic and chilli powder into a smooth paste in a liquidiser.

How to proceed

1. Heat the butter and fry the cinnamon, cloves and cardamoms for a few seconds.
2. Add the tomato paste and fry for 2 to 3 minutes.
3. Add the potatoes, cream, sugar and salt and cook for 5 to 6 minutes.

▶ **Serve hot** ◀

DILKUSH DAL

(Lentils/Pulses)

Dals which are rich in proteins, are equally important in a daily meal. Try Masala Dal with Potato Rotis or Rajma Curry with Onion Rotis. A combination of Yoghurt Curry with Coriander Roti is a real tempting one. Panchkuti Dal is an ideal dal for every day, since it is high in proteins.

MASALA DAL

A tasty combination of four dals.

Preparation time : 20 minutes. Cooking time : 30 minutes. Serves 4.

½ teacup moong dal
½ teacup masoor dal
½ teacup black gram (urad) dal
½ teacup toovar
(arhar) dal
3 onions, grated
2 tomatoes, chopped
3 tablespoons ghee
salt to taste
chopped coriander
for garnishing

To be ground into a paste
5 cloves garlic
2 teaspoons coriander seeds
1 teaspoon cumin seeds
¼ teaspoon turmeric powder
1 tablespoon chopped coriander
8 Kashmiri chillies
25 mm. piece ginger
3 sticks cinnamon
3 peppercorns
3 cloves

1. Wash all the dals together.
2. Add 4 teacups of water and cook until done in a pressure cooker.
3. Heat the ghee and fry the onions till light pink in colour.
4. Add the paste and fry for 3 to 4 minutes.
5. Add the tomatoes and fry again for 3 to 4 minutes.
6. Add the cooked dals and salt.
7. Cook for 5 to 7 minutes. Garnish with coriander.

▶ **Serve hot** ◀

RAJMA CURRY

A favourable from the Punjab.

Preparation time : 20 minutes. Cooking time : 20 minutes. Serves 6.

1 teacup red kidney beans (rajma)
2 onions, grated
1 teaspoon chilli powder
500 grams tomatoes
2 teaspoons sugar
3 tablespoons ghee
salt to taste

To be ground into a paste
7 cloves garlic
7 green chillies
25 mm. piece ginger

1. Soak the red kidney beans overnight.
2. Next day, cook in a pressure cooker. Drain.
3. Heat the ghee and fry the onions for 2 to 3 minutes.
Add the paste and chilli powder and fry again for 1 minute.
4. Add the cooked red kidney beans.
5. Cut the tomatoes into big pieces, add 2 teacups of water and cook.
When cooked, take out a thick soup through a sieve.
6. Add the tomato soup to the rajma mixture.
Add the sugar and salt.
7. Cook for a few minutes.

▶ **Serve hot** ◀

BROAD BEANS CURRY

Punjabi masala transforms this popular Gujarati dish.

Preparation time : 15 minutes. Cooking time : 20 minutes. Serves 6.

1½ teacups broad beans (Rangoon na val)
4 tomatoes
2 tablespoons ghee
salt to taste

For the paste

2 onions	2 teaspoons poppy seeds (khus-khus)
5 to 6 cloves garlic	4 to 5 peppercorns
6 Kashmiri chillies	4 to 5 cloves
3 teaspoons coriander seeds	2 to 3 sticks cinnamon
1 teaspoon cumin seeds	

For the paste

Burn the onions (with the skin on) on the gas until black.
Remove the outer skin and make a paste with the remaining ingredients.

1. Soak the beans overnight.
2. Next day, add 2 teacups of water and cook in a pressure cooker.
3. Cut the tomatoes into big pieces, add ½ teacup of water and cook.
When cooked, take out a purée by passing through a sieve.
4. Heat the ghee and fry the paste for 3 to 4 minutes.
5. Add the beans, tomato purée and salt and cook for a few minutes.

▶ **Serve hot with parathas** ◀

MIXED BEANS CURRY

With

POTATO BALLS

Makes a complete meal with puris or parathas.

Preparation time : 25 minutes. Cooking time : 35 minutes. Serves 6.

For the beans

½ teacup broad beans
(Rangoon na val)
½ teacup red kidney beans (rajma)
1 kg. tomatoes
1 onion, chopped
2 slit green chillies
1 teaspoon chilli powder
2 to 3 teaspoons sugar
1 tablespoon ghee
salt to taste

For the potato balls

4 potatoes, boiled and mashed
2 slices fresh bread
1 tablespoon chopped cashewnuts
or peanuts
3 to 4 green chillies, chopped
1 tablespoon chopped coriander
1 teaspoon lemon juice
oil for deep frying
salt to taste

For the beans

1. Soak the beans separately overnight.
2. Next day, cook each variety of beans separately in a pressure cooker. Drain.
3. Cut the tomatoes into big pieces, add ½ teacup of water and cook.
When cooked, take out a purée by passing through a sieve.
4. Heat the ghee and fry the onion for 1 minute.
5. Add the tomato purée, green chillies, chilli powder, sugar, salt and the cooked beans.
6 .Boil for at least 10 to 15 minutes.

For the potato balls

1. Dip the bread slices in water for 1 minute.
Squeeze out the water and crumble the bread.
2. Mix the crumbled bread with the remaining ingredients.
3. Shape into small balls and deep fry in hot oil.

How to serve

Just before serving, add the potato balls to the beans.

▶ **Serve hot** ◀

PANCHKUTI DAL

This delightful combination of five pulses is moderately spiced.

Preparation time : 15 minutes. Cooking time : 30 minutes. Serves 6 to 8.

1 tablespoon black gram (urad) dal
1 tablespoon toovar (arhar) dal
1 tablespoon moong dal
1 tablespoon gram (chana) dal
1 tablespoon masoor dal
1 teaspoon mustard seeds
1 teaspoon cumin seeds
12 mm. stick cinnamon
2 cloves
4 curry leaves

4 small red chillies
3 green chillies, finely chopped
2 teaspoons finely chopped ginger
2 teaspoons finely chopped garlic
2 tomatoes, roughly chopped
1/2 teaspoon garam masala,
page 125
2 tablespoons chopped coriander
juice of one lemon
2 tablespoons oil
salt to taste

1. Wash all the dals. Soak for 1 hour and then drain.
2. Add 5 teacups of water and cook in a pressure cooker until soft.
3. Heat the oil and fry the mustard seeds, cumin seeds, cinnamon and cloves until they begin to crackle.
4. Add the curry leaves, red chillies, green chillies, ginger and garlic and fry for 1 minute.
5. Add the tomatoes and garam masala, the dals, coriander, lemon juice and salt and boil for 8 to 10 minutes.

▶ **Serve hot** ◀

VEGETABLE

And

YOGHURT KADHI

A different style of kadhi.

Preparation time : 15 minutes. Cooking time : 20 minutes. Serves 6.

3 teacups mixed boiled vegetables
(carrots, french beans, cauliflower,
green peas)
3 teacups fresh curds
3 level tablespoons gram
flour (besan)
1 teaspoon mustard seeds
1 teaspoon cumin seeds

1 onion, chopped
1 teaspoon chilli powder
¼ teaspoon turmeric powder
¼ teaspoon coriander-cumin seed
(dhana-jira) powder
2 tablespoons chopped coriander
1 tablespoon ghee
salt to taste

1. Mix the curds and gram flour with 3 teacups of water and beat well.
2. Heat the ghee and fry the mustard seeds and cumin seeds until they begin to crackle.
3. Add the onion and fry for 1 minute.
4. Add the chilli powder, turmeric powder and coriander-cumin seed powder
and fry for 30 seconds.
5. Add the curds mixture and boil for 10 minutes, stirring for the first 3 minutes.
6. Add the vegetables and salt and cook for 3 minutes.

▶ *Sprinkle coriander leaves on top and serve hot* ◀

SPICY KOFTA KADHI

This tasty and unusual version of kadhi omits the dahi.

Preparation time : 15 minutes. Cooking time : 30 minutes. Serves 6.

For the kadhi

1 stick cinnamon
3 cloves
2 cardamoms
½ teaspoon chilli powder
2 level tablespoons gram
flour (besan)

½ teacup tamarind water,
refer sambar recipe, (page 73, step 4)
2 tablespoons fresh cream
2 tablespoons ghee
salt to taste

To be ground into a paste
(for the kadhi)

2 tablespoons poppy seeds
(khus-khus)
2 tablespoons cashewnuts
6 to 8 cloves garlic
25 mm. piece ginger
4 green chillies
2 tomatoes
1 tablespoon grated coconut

For the koftas

4 tablespoons aubergines (brinjals),
finely chopped
1 onion, finely chopped
½ teacup grated cabbage
2 green chillies, finely chopped
4 level tablespoons gram
flour (besan)
¼ teaspoon baking powder
oil for deep frying
salt to taste

For the koftas
1. Mix all the ingredients for the koftas except the oil and add a
little water to make a batter.
2. Heat the oil and when hot, drop teaspoonfuls of the batter in it.
Fry for about 3 minutes until golden brown.
3. Repeat with the remaining batter.

For the kadhi
1. Heat the ghee and fry the cinnamon, cloves and cardamoms for a few seconds.
2. Add the paste and chilli powder and fry for 2 minutes.
3. Add the gram flour and fry again for 1 minute.
4. Add 3 teacups of water, the tamarind water and salt and boil for 5 minutes.
5. Just before serving, add the koftas and the cream and give one boil.

▶ **Serve hot** ◀

SAMBAR

This variation of the popular South Indian dish goes very well with idlis.

Preparation time : 15 minutes. Cooking time : 30 minutes. Serves 6 to 8.

1½ teacups toovar (arhar) dal
200 grams white pumpkin
(lauki), cut into big pieces
6 to 8 pieces drumsticks (optional)
1 teaspoon mustard seeds
1 teaspoon fenugreek (methi) seeds
6 to 7 curry leaves
2 pinches asafoetida

2 tablespoons sambhar powder
7 small sambhar onions
2 tablespoons tamarind
1 tablespoon chopped coriander
1 large or 2 medium tomatoes, quartered
2 tablespoons oil
salt to taste

1. Wash the dal thoroughly and add 4 teacups of water.
2. Pressure cook the dal until soft. Blend the cooked dal in a mixer.
3. Boil the pumpkin with the drumsticks in 1½ teacups of water.
Drain and add to the dal. If you like, boil the onions with the pumpkin.
4. Soak the tamarind in a little water and keep aside for 30 minutes.
Rub the tamarind by hand and strain. Add to the dal mixture.
5. Heat the oil and fry the mustard seeds and fenugreek seeds until they begin to crackle.
Add the curry leaves and fry for 2 to 3 minutes.
6. Add the asafoetida, cooked dal mixture, sambhar powder and coriander.
7. Add salt and boil for 5 to 7 minutes.
8. Add the tomatoes and boil again for 2 to 3 minutes.

▶ **Serve hot** ◀

CORN AND VEGETABLE RING

With

COCONUT CURRY

Picture on page 83

Try this novel dish for a party.

Preparation time : 30 minutes. Cooking time : 35 minutes. Serves 6.

For the corn and vegetable ring
2 teacups cooked corn
2 potatoes, boiled and mashed
2 teacups mixed boiled vegetables (french beans, carrots, green peas)
1 teacup cooked rice
1 tomato, sliced
1 capsicum, sliced
2 teaspoons mustard seeds
2 pinches asafoetida
4 teaspoons sesame seeds
4 tablespoons chopped cashewnuts
6 tablespoons oil
salt to taste

To be ground into a paste (for the corn and vegetable ring)
1 teacup chopped coriander
6 green chillies
25 mm. piece ginger
4 tablespoons grated coconut
juice of one lemon
1 teaspoon sugar
1 teaspoon salt

§

For the coconut curry
1 coconut
1 teaspoon cumin seeds
1 slit green chilli
a few curry leaves
1/2 teaspoon sugar
2 tablespoons ghee
salt to taste

To be ground into a paste (for the coconut curry)
2 tablespoons grated coconut
1 onion
5 green chillies
1 tablespoon chopped coriander
12 mm. piece ginger

74

For the corn and vegetable ring

1. Crush the corn lightly.
2. Mix the potatoes, vegetables, rice and corn. Add the paste and salt and mix well.
3. Heat 3 tablespoons of oil, add half the mustard seeds and fry until they begin to crackle. Add half the sesame seeds and half the cashewnuts and fry for a few seconds.
4. Add the vegetable mixture and mix well.
5. Arrange the tomato and capsicum slices at the bottom of a greased ring mould tin.
6. Fill the mould with the vegetable mixture. Cover and bake in a hot oven at 200°C (400°F) for 15 minutes.
7. When you want to serve, unmould the ring mould on a serving dish.
8. Heat the remaining oil, add the remaining mustard seeds and fry until they begin to crackle. Add the asafoetida and the remaining sesame seeds and cashewnuts and fry for a few seconds. Pour this mixture over the corn and vegetable ring.

For the coconut curry

1. Grate the coconut. Add 3 teacups of water and blend in a mixer. Strain and take out coconut milk.
2. Heat the ghee and fry the cumin seeds until they begin to crackle. Add the green chilli and curry leaves and fry again for a little while.
3. Add the paste and fry again for 1 minute.
4. Add the coconut milk, sugar and salt and boil for 10 minutes.

▶ *Serve hot with the corn and vegetable ring* ◀

SAVOURY CAKE

In

COCONUT SAUCE

Picture on page 65

Idli and coconut sauce make a delightful combination.

Preparation time : 15 minutes. Cooking time : 20 minutes. Serves 6.

For the savoury cake

2 packets (200 grams each) idli mix or khatta dhokla mix
2 tablespoons mixed boiled vegetables (carrots, french beans, green peas)

For the coconut sauce
1 coconut
1 level teaspoon cornflour
½ teaspoon cumin seeds
2 curry leaves
2 green chillies, slit
1 teaspoon lemon juice
1 tablespoon ghee
½ teaspoon sugar
salt to taste

To be ground into a paste (for the coconut sauce)
2 green chillies
25 mm. piece ginger
2 tablespoons chopped coriander

For the savoury cake
1. Prepare the idli batter or khatta dhokla batter as per instructions given on the packet.
2. Pour the batter into a greased 150 or 175 mm. flan tin and steam for 15 minutes.

For the coconut sauce
1. Grate the coconut. Add 4 teacups of water to the grated coconut and blend in a mixer. Strain and take out coconut milk. Add the cornflour and mix well.
2. Heat the ghee and fry the cumin seeds until they begin to crackle. Add the curry leaves and green chillies and fry again for a few seconds.
3. Add the paste and fry for a few seconds.
4. Add the coconut milk and boil for 4 to 5 minutes. Add the lemon juice, sugar and salt.

How to proceed
1. Invert the flan tin on an ovenproof dish.
2. Just before serving, pour the coconut sauce over the moulded cake and bake in a hot oven at 200°C (400° F) for 10 minutes.

 ▶ *Serve hot* ◀

CHAAWAL LA JAWAAB

(Rice dishes)

This section presents a selection of rice dishes
from different regions and styles, such as
Cabbage Rice from Maharashtra, Biryanis in
the Hyderabadi style, Vegetable Pullao in the
Moghlai style and Khichadi in Bengali style.
Each has its own unique flavour and gives the
satisfaction of a perfect meal.

BOHRI KHICHADI

> *Rice and dal cooked with Bohri masala.*

Preparation time : 20 minutes. Cooking time : 30 minutes. Serves 6.

For the khichadi
2 teacups uncooked rice
1 teacup toovar (arhar) dal
3 pinches saffron (optional)
salt to taste

For the gravy
1 onion, chopped
1 teaspoon garam masala, page 125
1 teacup fresh curds
1 teaspoon sugar
3 tablespoons ghee
salt to taste

To be ground into a paste (for the gravy)
5 red chillies
2 green chillies
1½ onions
4 cloves garlic
1½ teaspoons cumin seeds

Other ingredients
2 large sliced onions (deep fried in ghee)
2 tablespoons ghee

For the khichadi
1. Boil the rice. Each grain of the cooked rice should be separate. Drain and cool.
2. Cook the dal in 2 teacups of water. Cool.
3. Mix the cooked rice and dal. Add salt.
4. Warm the saffron in a small vessel, add a little water and rub until the saffron dissolves. Add to the khichadi and mix well.

For the gravy
1. Heat the ghee and fry the onion for 1 minute.
2. Add the paste and fry again for 2 minutes.
3. Add the garam masala and fry again for a little time.
4. Remove from the fire. Add the curds, sugar and salt. Mix well.

How to proceed
1. Put 2 tablespoons of ghee at the bottom of a baking bowl. Sprinkle a few fried onions. Spread half of the khichadi. Next spread the above gravy. Finally, spread the remaining khichadi mixed with the balance fried onions.
2. Cover and bake in a hot oven at 230°C (450°F) for 15 minutes.

▶ **Serve hot** ◀

THREE-IN-ONE RICE

A three layered pullao with contrasting tastes.

Preparation time : 25 minutes. Cooking time : 35 minutes. Serves 8.

For the orange rice

1 teacup uncooked rice
2 to 3 tomatoes
1 onion, chopped
2 carrots, grated
2 green chillies, chopped
1 teaspoon sugar
2 tablespoons ghee
salt to taste

For the white rice

1 teacup uncooked rice
1/2 teaspoon shah-jira
2 green chillies, chopped
100 grams chopped paneer
2 tablespoons ghee
salt to taste

For the green rice

1 teacup uncooked rice
1 onion, chopped
1 teacup boiled green peas
2 tablespoons ghee
salt to taste

To be ground into a paste (for the green rice)

1 teacup chopped coriander
4 green chillies
4 cloves garlic
25 mm. piece ginger
juice of 1/2 lemon

For the orange rice

1. Boil the rice. Each grain of the cooked rice should be separate. Drain and cool.
2. Cut the tomatoes into big pieces, add 2 tablespoons of water and cook. When cooked, take out a thick purée by passing through a sieve.
3. Heat the ghee and fry the onion for 1 minute.
4. Add the carrots and fry again for 1 minute.
5. Add the tomato purée, green chillies, sugar and salt and cook again for 2 minutes.
6. Add the rice and mix well.

For the white rice

1. Boil the rice. Each grain of the cooked rice should be separate. Drain and cool.
2. Heat the ghee and fry the shah-jira until they begin to crackle.
3. Add the rice, green chillies, paneer and salt and mix well.

For the green rice

1. Boil the rice. Each grain of the cooked rice should be separate. Drain and cool.
2. Heat the ghee and fry the onion for 1 minute.
3. Add the paste and fry again for 2 minutes.
4. Add the rice, green peas and salt and mix well.

How to proceed

1. In a large cake tin, spread the three different coloured rice in any desired sequence.
2. Cover and steam for 15 minutes.
3. Invert on a serving plate.

▶ **Serve hot** ◀

VEGETABLE

And

LENTIL PULLAO

Rich and tasty.

Preparation time : 20 minutes. Cooking time : 35 minutes. Serves 6.

For the rice
1½ teacups uncooked rice
1 teacup toovar (arhar) dal
2 pinches saffron
1 teacup mixed boiled vegetables
(french beans, carrots, green peas)
1 onion, sliced and fried
salt to taste

For the curry
1½ teacups fresh curds
1 teaspoon sugar
3 tablespoons ghee
salt to taste

To be ground into a paste (for the curry)
1 onion
2 tablespoons grated fresh coconut
8 Kashmiri chillies
25 mm. piece ginger
4 cloves garlic
3 teaspoons poppy seeds (khus-khus)
3 cardamoms
2 teaspoons coriander seeds
1 teaspoon cumin seeds

Other ingredients
1 tablespoon ghee
1 onion, sliced and fried
fresh curds for serving

For the rice

1. Boil the rice. Each grain of the cooked rice should be separate. Drain and cool.
2. Cook the dal in 2 teacups of water. Cool.
3. Warm the saffron in a small vessel, add a little water and rub until the saffron dissolves.
4. Mix the rice, dal, saffron, vegetables, fried onion and salt and keep aside.

For the curry

1. Heat the ghee and fry the paste for 3 to 4 minutes.
2. Remove from the heat and add the curds, sugar and salt.

How to proceed

1. Put 1 tablespoon of ghee at the bottom of a large baking bowl.
2. Spread some fried onion slices on it and make layers of rice and curry. Sprinkle the balance onion slices on top.
3. Cover and bake in a hot oven at 230°C (450°F) for 20 minutes. Just before serving, turn upside down on a serving dish.

▶ **Serve hot with curds** ◀

FRUIT
And
VEGETABLE PULLAO

Picture on page 84

A royal Moghlai style pullao with fruits and vegetables.

Preparation time : 20 minutes. Cooking time : 40 minutes. Serves 6.

For the rice

1½ teacups uncooked rice
2 pinches saffron
1 teaspoon milk
½ teaspoon shah-jira
2 sticks cinnamon
2 cloves
2 cardamoms
1 teacup boiled green peas
8 to 10 dried apricots,
soaked in water for 1 hour
3 tablespoons ghee
salt to taste

For the paneer koftas

200 grams crumbled
paneer
3 tablespoons
plain flour (maida)
a pinch soda bi-carb
2 tablespoons
chopped coriander
2 green chillies, chopped
salt to taste
ghee for deep frying

For the gravy

1 teacup fresh curds
½ teaspoon sugar
3 tablespoons ghee
salt to taste

To be ground into a paste (for the gravy)

1 onion	2 sticks cinnamon
3 tablespoons grated fresh coconut	3 cloves
5 cloves garlic	3 cardamoms
2 teaspoons coriander seeds	2 teaspoons poppy seeds (khus-khus)
1 teaspoon cumin seeds	7 to 8 red chillies
	25 mm. piece ginger

For baking

2 tablespoons ghee

For the rice

1. Boil the rice. Each grain of the cooked rice should be separate. Drain and cool.
2. Warm the saffron in a small vessel, add the milk and rub until the saffron dissolves. Add to the rice.
3. Heat the ghee, add the shah-jira, cinnamon, cloves and cardamoms and fry until they begin to crackle. Add the rice, green peas and salt and cook for a few minutes.
4. Add the apricot pieces.

For the paneer koftas

1. Mix all the ingredients and shape into small round balls.
2. Deep fry in ghee.

For the gravy

1. Heat the ghee and fry the paste for 3 to 4 minutes.
2. Remove from the heat and add the curds, sugar and salt.

How to proceed

1. Add the paneer koftas to the rice.
2. In a large baking bowl, put 2 tablespoons of ghee at the bottom. Make layers by spreading ⅓ of the rice, then spreading ½ of the gravy, next spreading a further ⅓ of the rice and finally spreading the remaining gravy and rice.
3. Cover and bake in a hot oven at 230°C (450°F) for 20 minutes.

▶ *Just before serving, turn upside down on a big serving plate and serve hot* ◀

Corn and Vegetable Ring with Coconut Curry–Page 74

KORMA RICE

Rich but not too spicy!

Preparation time : 25 minutes. Cooking time : 45 minutes. Serves 4.

For the rice
1½ teacups uncooked rice
2 bay leaves
2 sticks cinnamon
2 cardamoms
2 cloves
2 pinches turmeric powder
2 tablespoons ghee
salt to taste

For the korma
2 teacups moong sprouts
2 tomatoes
2 onions, grated
1 teaspoon coriander-cumin seed
(dhana-jira) powder
1 teaspoon chilli powder
½ teaspoon sugar
1 teacup milk
2 tablespoons fresh cream
3 tablespoons ghee
salt to taste

To be ground into paste no. 1 (for the korma)
3 cloves garlic
12 mm. piece giner
2 cardamoms

To be ground into paste no. 2 (for the korma)
1 tablespoon cashewnuts
1 tablespoon poppy seeds (khus-khus)

For baking
1 tablespoon ghee

For the rice
1. Heat the ghee and fry the bay leaves, cinnamon, cardamoms and cloves for ½ minute.
2. Add the rice, turmeric powder, salt and 4 to 5 teacups of water and cook.
3. When the rice is cooked, drain and cool.
Each grain of the cooked rice should be separate.

For the korma
1. Boil the tomatoes in hot water. After 10 minutes, remove the skin and chop.
2. Heat the ghee and fry the onion until light pink in colour.
Add paste no.1, the coriander-cumin seed powder and chilli powder and fry for 1 minute.
Add the tomatoes and fry for 3 to 4 minutes.
3. Add the moong sprouts, ¼ teacup of water,
the sugar and salt and cook for a few minutes.
4. In another vessel, mix the milk, cream and paste no.2.
Add this mixture to the korma and cook for a few minutes.

Top: Fruit and Vegetable Raita–Page 22, Bottom: Fruit and Vegetable Pullao –Page 81

How to proceed

1. Put 1 tablespoon of ghee at the bottom of a baking bowl and build up alternate layers (2 to 3 each depending on the bowl size) of rice and korma, beginning and ending with rice.
2. Cover and bake in a hot oven at 230°C (450°F) for 20 minutes.

▶ *Just before serving, turn upside down on a serving plate and serve hot* ◀

BAKED RICE

With

GREEN CURRY

Green masala makes this a tastier rice.

Preparation time : 25 minutes. Cooking time : 35 minutes. Serves 6.

For the rice
1½ teacups uncooked rice
½ teaspoon shah-jira
2 sticks cinnamon
2 cloves
2 tablespoons ghee
salt to taste

For the curry
1 teacup boiled green peas
2 cardamoms
150 grams paneer,
cut into small pieces
¾ teacup fresh curds
½ teaspoon sugar
2 tablespoons ghee
salt to taste

To be ground into a paste (for the curry)
1 teacup chopped coriander
7 green chillies
1 onion
4 cloves garlic
25 mm. piece ginger
1 tablespoon fresh mint
1 tablespoon poppy seeds (khus-khus)
juice of ½ lemon

For baking
1 tablespoon ghee

For decoration
boiled green peas
potato salis

For the rice

1. Boil the rice. Each grain of the cooked rice should be separate. Drain and cool.
2. Heat the ghee, add the shah-jira, cinnamon and cloves
and fry until they begin to crackle.
3. Add the rice and salt.

For the curry

1. Heat the ghee, add the paste and cardamoms and fry for 2 minutes.
Remove from the heat.
2. Add the green peas, paneer, curds, sugar and salt and mix well.

How to proceed

1. Put 1 tablespoon of ghee at the bottom of a large baking bowl.
Make layers by spreading 1/3 of the rice, then spreading 1/2 of the curry,
next spreading a further 1/3 of the rice and finally spreading the remaining curry and rice.
2. Cover and bake in a hot oven at 230°C (450°F) for 20 minutes.

How to serve

1. Just before serving, turn upside down on a big serving plate.
2. Surround with green peas and sprinkle potato salis on the top and sides.

▶ **Serve hot** ◀

SPICY KHICHADI

With

CURRY SAUCE

A simple khichadi with rich curry sauce.

Preparation time : 20 minutes. Cooking time : 25 minutes. Serves 6.

For the khichadi

3/4 teacup masoor dal
2 teacups uncooked rice
3 tablespoons ghee
salt to taste

To be ground into a paste (for the khichadi)

3 tablespoons grated coconut
5 cloves garlic
2 teaspoons coriander seeds
1 teaspoon cumin seeds
4 cardamoms
25 mm. piece ginger
6 Kashmiri chillies
½ teaspoon turmeric powder

For the curry sauce

3 tomatoes
1 teaspoon sugar
2 pinches saffron
¼ teaspoon milk
4 tablespoons ghee
salt to taste

To be ground into a paste (for the curry sauce)

2 onions
1 tablespoon cashewnuts
1 tablespoon almonds (optional)
1 tablespoon coriander seeds
1 tablespoon poppy seeds (khus-khus)
2 tablespoons aniseed (saunf)
2 tablespoons grated fresh coconut
25 mm. piece ginger
2 green chillies
4 red chillies
3 cardamoms
3 cloves
3 sticks cinnamon
7 curry leaves

For the khichadi

1. Soak the masoor dal in water overnight.
2. Next day, cook in salted water. When cooked, drain the water.
3. Boil the rice. Each grain of the cooked rice should be separate. Drain and cool.
4. Heat the ghee and fry the paste for 3 to 4 minutes.
5. Add the rice, dal and salt and cook for 2 minutes.

For the curry sauce

1. Cut the tomatoes into big pieces, add 1½ teacups of water and cook.
When cooked, take out a purée by passing through a sieve.
2. Heat the ghee and fry the paste for at least 4 minutes.
3. Add the tomato purée, sugar and salt.
4. Warm the saffron in a small vessel, add the milk and rub until the saffron dissolves.
Add to the curry sauce.

▶ *Serve the hot rice separately with curry sauce* ◀

NOTE: Both the khichadi and the curry sauce can be served by themselves separately.

VEGETABLE BIRYANI

A rich Moghlai pullao layered with curry.

Preparation time : 15 minutes. Cooking time : 40 minutes. Serves 4.

1½ teacups uncooked rice
2 pinches saffron
2 onions, sliced
2 tablespoons cashewnuts,
broken into pieces
2 tablespoons raisins
3 tomatoes, finely chopped
2 capsicums, sliced
2 teacups mixed boiled vegetables
(cauliflower, carrots, potatoes,
green peas)
1 tablespoon chopped coriander
a little milk
4 tablespoons ghee
salt to taste

To be ground into a paste
6 cloves garlic
25 mm. piece ginger
3 cardamoms
4 green chillies
3 cloves
1 tablespoon poppy seeds
(khus-khus)
2 sticks cinnamon
½ teaspoon
turmeric powder
½ teaspoon
chilli powder
2 onions
6 mint leaves

For baking
2 tablespoons ghee

1. Boil the rice. Each grain of the cooked rice should be separate. Drain and cool.
2. Warm the saffron in a small vessel, add a little water and rub until it dissolves.
3. Add the saffron liquid and salt to the cooked rice. Mix well.
4. Heat the ghee and fry the onions until brown.
Remove the onions and in the same ghee, add the cashewnuts and raisins
and fry for a few seconds. Remove and keep aside for decoration.
5. In the same ghee, add the paste and fry for 3 to 4 minutes.
Add the tomatoes and capsicum and fry again for 2 to 3 minutes.
If you like, sprinkle a little water. Add the boiled vegetables
and coriander and cook for a while.

How to proceed
1. Put 2 tablespoons of ghee at the bottom of a baking bowl.
Make layers of the rice and vegetables, beginning and ending with rice.
2. Sprinkle a little milk on top. Cover and bake in a hot oven
at 200°C (400°F) for 15 to 20 minutes.

▶ *Just before serving, turn upside down on a serving plate,*
garnish with fried onions, cashewnuts and raisins and serve hot ◀

CORN PULLAO

Looks colourful, tastes beautiful!

Preparation time : 15 minutes. Cooking time : 40 minutes. Serves 6.

For the rice

1 teacup uncooked rice
1 teacup cooked corn
2 sticks cinnamon
2 cloves
1 capsicum, chopped
1 boiled carrot, chopped
2 tablespoons ghee
salt to taste

For the curry

1 teacup fresh curds
2 tablespoons fresh cream
½ teaspoon sugar
2 tablespoons ghee
salt to taste

For the paste (for the curry)

1 onion, chopped
2 tablespoons grated coconut
5 cloves garlic
2 teaspoons coriander seeds
1 teaspoon cumin seeds
2 sticks cinnamon
2 cloves
2 cardamoms
25mm. piece ginger
2 teaspoons poppy seeds (khus-khus)
6 red chillies

For the rice

1. Boil the rice. Each grain of the cooked rice should be separate. Drain and cool.
2. Heat the ghee and fry the cinnamon and cloves for ½ minute.
3. Add the rice, corn, capsicum, carrot and salt and cook for 1 minute.

For the curry

1. Heat the ghee and fry the paste for 3 to 4 minutes.
2. Add the curds, cream, sugar, salt and ½ teacup of water and cook for a few seconds.

How to proceed

1. On a large sheet of aluminum foil, spread alternate layers of rice and curry
so that there are 3 layers of rice with 2 layers of curry in-between.
2. Make a packet of the foil and bake in a hot oven at 230°C (450°F) for 20 minutes.

▶ **Unwrap and serve hot** ◀

CABBAGE RICE

A delicately flavoured rice dish.

Preparation time : 10 minutes. Cooking time : 20 minutes. Serves 4.

1 teacup uncooked rice
1 onion, grated
½ teacup shredded cabbage
1 capsicum, sliced

½ teaspoon pepper powder
2 tablespoons butter
salt to taste
2 tablespoons grated cheese

1. Boil the rice. Each grain of the cooked rice should be separate. Drain and cool.
2. Heat the butter and fry the onion for 2 to 3 minutes.
3. Add the cabbage and capsicum and cook for 2 to 3 minutes.
4. Add the rice, pepper and salt.

▶ **Sprinkle the cheese on top and serve hot** ◀

PULSES PULLAO

A protein packed pullao!

Preparation time : 15 minutes. Cooking time : 20 minutes. Serves 6 to 8.

1½ teacups uncooked rice
2 tablespoons black-eyed
beans (lobhia)
2 tablespoons chick peas
(Kabuli chana)
2 tablespoons peanuts
1 teaspoon mustard seeds

2 onions, chopped
2 tomatoes, chopped
1 teaspoon chilli powder
1 teaspoon garam masala, page125
2 teaspoons lemon juice
5 tablespoons oil
salt to taste

1. Soak the black-eyed beans, chick peas and peanuts for at least 6 to 7 hours.
Then, boil together until cooked. Drain.
2. Boil the rice. Each grain of the cooked rice should be separate. Drain and cool.
3. Heat the oil and fry the mustard seeds until they begin to crackle.
4. Add the onions and tomatoes and fry for 1 minute.
Add the chilli powder and garam masala and fry again for a few minutes.
Add the cooked beans, chick peas, peanuts, rice, the lemon juice and salt Mix well.

▶ **Serve hot** ◀

KHICHADI – BENGALI STYLE

A spicy khichadi with vegetables.

Preparation time : 15 minutes. Cooking time : 30 minutes. Serves 6 to 8.

1½ teacups uncooked rice
1 onion, chopped
2 sticks cinnamon
4 cloves
3 cardamoms
2 bay leaves
1 teacup masoor dal
8 small potatoes
6 to 7 small onions, peeled

10 to 12 french beans,
cut into small pieces
1 teacup green peas
3 green chillies, chopped
½ teaspoon turmeric powder
4 cloves garlic
25 mm. piece ginger,
finely chopped or grated
4 tablespoons ghee
salt to taste

1. Crush the cinnamon, cloves and cardamoms lightly.
2. Heat 2 tablespoons of ghee and fry the chopped onion for a few minutes.
Add the crushed spices and bay leaves and fry for a few seconds.
3. Add the rice, masoor dal, potatoes, small onions, french beans, green peas,
green chillies, turmeric powder, garlic and ginger. Mix well and cook for 2 minutes.
4. Add 5 teacups of hot water and salt. Cover and cook for 20 to 25 minutes
or until the vegetables are soft.
5. Remove from the heat; pour the remaining ghee on top.

▶ **Serve hot** ◀

*Anti-clockwise from top : Semolina and Vermicelli Idlis, Page-102 ,
Malbari Curry–Page 60 , Coconut Chutney–Page 25*

SWAADBHARA NAASHTA

(Snacks)

The hot snacks in this section are ideal accompaniments for drinks and also for breakfast or tea parties. For example, Vegetable Kababs, Papad Potato Rolls and Cabbage Wadas go well with cocktails. You can serve Semolina Pancakes, Quick Bread Snack or Semolina and Vermicelli Idlis/Uttapas for breakfast. Whereas for a tea party, consider serving Spicy Chaat – Calcutta Style, Green Peas Renedy or Quick Green Peas Snack.

SEMOLINA PANCAKES

Picture on page 65

If you plan ahead, this snack is very easy to make.

Preparation time : 10 minutes. Cooking time : 15 minutes. Makes about 18 pancakes.

2 teacups semolina (sooji)
1 teacup fresh curds
1 teacup cooked corn or
1 teacup finely chopped cabbage
2 green chillies, chopped

½ teaspoon soda bi-carb
2 teaspoons melted ghee or oil
2 pinches asafoetida
salt to taste

For cooking
ghee

For garnish
1 carrot, grated
2 tablespoons chopped coriander

For serving
coconut chutney, page 25

1. Mix the semolina and curds with 1 teacup of water
   and keep aside for at least 5 to 6 hours.
2. Add the remaining ingredients and mix very well.
3. Prepare small pancakes on a non-stick frying pan (griddle) using a little ghee.
   Sprinkle grated carrot and coriander while cooking.

▶ **Serve hot with coconut chutney** ◀

QUICK BREAD SNACK

A lovely bread based snack.

Preparation time : 15 minutes. Cooking time : 5 minutes. Serves 4.

10 to 12 bread slices
2 teaspoons mustard seeds
2 onions, chopped
2 curry leaves
2 tomatoes, chopped
4 to 5 green chillies, chopped

1 teaspoon finely chopped ginger
2 tablespoons tomato ketchup
juice of 1 lemon (approx.)
2 tablespoons chopped coriander
2 tablespoons oil
salt to taste

1. Soak the bread slices in a little water for a few minutes.
Squeeze out the water and crumble thoroughly.
2. Heat the oil and fry the mustard seeds until they begin to crackle.
Add the onions and curry leaves and fry again until the onions are light pink in colour.
3. Add the tomatoes, green chillies and ginger and cook for 1 minute.
4. Add the crumbled bread, tomato ketchup, lemon juice,
coriander and salt and cook for 1 minute.

▶ *Serve hot* ◀

VEGETABLE KABABS

These spicy kababs are ideal for cocktails.

Preparation time : 25 minutes. Cooking time : 15 minutes. Serves 4.

500 grams grated white
pumpkin (lauki)
2 onions, grated
2 medium sized boiled
potatoes, grated

3 level tablespoons
gram flour (besan)
2 tablespoons chopped coriander
5 green chillies, chopped
1 teaspoon shah-jira
salt to taste

For cooking
oil for deep frying

To be mixed into a masala mixture (for serving)
1 teaspoon chilli powder
1 teaspoon amchur powder
1/2 teaspoon salt
2 onions, finely chopped

1. Sprinkle 2 teaspoons of salt on the grated vegetables and leave for 20 minutes.
Squeeze out the water.
2. Add the remaining ingredients and shape into small round balls.
3. Deep fry in hot oil.
4. Whilst the balls are hot, press them flat.

▶ *Sprinkle the masala mixture on top and serve hot* ◀

GREEN PEAS RENEDY

Colourful and spicy.

Preparation time : 20 minutes. Cooking time : 15 minutes. Serves 6.

For the green peas mixture

4 teacups green peas
5 green chillies, finely chopped
2 pinches soda bi-carb
juice of 2 lemons
1 ½ teaspoons (approx.) sugar
3 teaspoons oil
salt to taste

For the paneer balls

150 grams grated paneer, page 126
¼ teaspoon green chillies
1 level teaspoon cornflour
salt to taste

For the potato puris

5 potatoes, boiled and mashed
4 green chillies, finely chopped
¼ teaspoon turmeric powder
1 ½ teaspoons sugar
salt to taste
3 teaspoons oil

§

For cooking

1 level teacup plain flour (maida)
bread crumbs
oil for deep frying

For serving

tomato sauce

For the green peas mixture

1. Mash the green peas with the green chillies.
2. Heat the oil, add the green peas mixture, soda bi-carb, lemon juice,
sugar and salt and cook for 2 minutes.
3. Cool.

For the paneer balls

1. Mash the paneer with the green chillies, cornflour and salt.
2. Shape into small round balls.

For the potato puris

1. Mash the potatoes with the green chillies.
Add the turmeric powder, sugar and salt and mix well.
2. Heat the oil, add the potato mixture and cook for 1 minute.
3. Cool. Divide the mixture into 6 portions.
4. Roll out each portion into a thin round of about 100 mm. diameter.

How to proceed

1. Put a paneer ball in each potato round and fold to cover the paneer ball completely.
2. Cover the paneer potato puri balls with the green peas mixture. Press very well.
3. Mix the flour in 1½ teacups of water. Dip the balls in this mixture. Roll into bread crumbs and deep fry in hot oil.

▶ *Cut each ball into two and serve hot with tomato sauce* ◀

CORN PANCAKES

An ideal snack when corn is in season.

Preparation time : 10 minutes. Cooking time : 25 minutes. Makes 15 to 20 pancakes.

12 fresh tender corncobs
4 level tablespoons
plain flour (maida)
¼ teaspoon baking powder

4 tablespoons fresh cream
4 tablespoons milk
1 tablespoon chopped coriander
3 to 4 green chillies, chopped
salt to taste

For cooking
corn leaves
ghee

For serving
butter
grated cheese
green chutney, page 25

1. Boil the corncobs. Remove the corn with a sharp knife and grind coarsely.
2. Add the remaining ingredients and mix well.
3. Spread about 1 tablespoon of the mixture on half portion of a corn leaf and fold the other part of the leaf on top.
4. Cook on a hot tawa (griddle) on both sides using a little ghee.

▶ *Serve hot with butter, cheese and chutney* ◀

CABBAGE WADAS

You will enjoy this delicious combination of lentil and vegetables.

Preparation time : 15 minutes. Cooking time : 15 minutes. Makes 10 to 12 wadas.

450 grams gram (chana) dal

7 to 8 green chillies

2 teacups shredded cabbage

1 carrot, finely chopped

1 onion, finely chopped

2 tablespoons chopped coriander

salt to taste

oil for deep frying

To serve
green chutney, page 25

1. Soak the gram dal overnight.
2. Next day, keep aside ½ teacup of the gram dal.
Grind the rest of the gram dal coarsely along with the green chillies.
3. Add the cabbage, carrot, onion, coriander and salt and the remaining gram dal.
4. Shape into small thick cakes of about 50 mm. diameter and deep fry in hot oil.

▶ *Serve hot with green chutney* ◀

PAPAD POTATO ROLLS

Picture on page 94

> A delicious snack made from the lowly papads.

Preparation time : 30 minutes. Cooking time : 20 minutes. Makes 20 to 25 rolls.

8 to 10 papads

4 potatoes, boiled

2 green chillies, finely chopped

½ teaspoon chilli powder

juice of 1 lemon

2 tablespoons chopped coriander

½ teaspoon garam masala, page 125

½ teaspoon sugar

salt to taste

Other ingredients
a few tablespoons gram flour (besan)
oil for deep frying

1. Mash the potatoes. Add the green chillies, chilli powder, lemon juice, coriander, garam masala, sugar and salt and mix well.
2. Divide the potato mixture into several portions and shape each portion into a long roll of about the same length as the diameter of the papads.
3. Dip the papads in water for a few seconds.
4. Put a potato roll on the corner of each papad and roll up.
5. Seal the edges with a paste made of equal volumes of gram flour and water.
6. Deep fry in hot oil until golden brown.

▶ *Cut into small pieces and serve hot* ◀

SPINACH PAKODA CHAAT

A different type of chaat.

Preparation time : 10 minutes. Cooking time : 10 minutes. Serves 6.

10 to 15 fresh spinach leaves
¾ teacup gram flour (besan)
½ teaspoon chilli powder
salt to taste
oil for deep frying

For serving
sweet chutney, page 24
chilli powder
cumin seed powder
fresh curds
oil for frying

1. Mix the gram flour, chilli powder, salt and enough water to make a thick batter.
2. Dip a few spinach leaves at a time into the batter.
Drop them in hot oil and deep fry until crisp.
3. Place the hot pakodas on a serving plate.

▶ *Serve with sweet chutney, chilli powder, cumin seed powder and fresh curds* ◀

QUICK SPICY SNACK

For this delicious chaat bhel, adjust the chutney, curds and powders to suit to your taste.

Preparation time : 20 minutes. No cooking. Serves 3 to 4.

3 to 4 teacups papadis, page 106
3 tablespoons chopped pineapple
3 boiled potatoes,
cut into small pieces
3 tablespoons finely chopped
raw mango
4 tablespoons cooked chick peas
(Kabuli chana)

For topping
sweet chutney, page 24
green chutney, page 25
fresh curds
roasted cumin seed powder
roasted chilli powder
chaat masala, page 125
salt to taste

1. Keep aside a few papadis for decoration and crush the remaining papadis.
2. Add the pineapple, potatoes, raw mango, chick peas, sweet chutney,
green chutney, curds and salt and mix.
3. Sprinkle the cumin seed powder, chilli powder and chaat masala on the mixture.

▶ *Arrange a few papadis on top and serve* ◀

POTATO SNACK

Ideal for cocktail parties.

Preparation time : 5 minutes. Cooking time : 20 minutes. Serves 8 to 10.

½ kg. small round potatoes, boiled

To be ground into a paste

20 to 30 fresh mint leaves
3 tablespoons chopped coriander
2 green chillies
12 mm. piece ginger
1 teaspoon lemon juice
2 teaspoons chaat masala, page 125
salt to taste

1. Peel the potatoes.
2. Apply the paste all over the potatoes. Taste and adjust the spices if necessary.

▶ **Serve cold on tooth-picks** ◀

SEMOLINA

And

VERMICELLI IDLIS

Picture on page 93

This popular South Indian style snack is quick and easy to prepare.

Preparation time : 15 minutes. Cooking time : 30 minutes. Serves 4 to 6.

1 teacup semolina (sooji)
2 teacups vermicelli, broken
2 tablespoons cashewnuts,
    cut into small pieces
1 teacup beaten curds
4 tablespoons oil
salt to taste

§

For the tempering

2 teaspoons black gram
    (urad) dal
1 teaspoon mustard seeds
5 to 6 finely chopped green chillies
3 to 4 curry leaves
1 tablespoon oil

For serving

coconut chutney, page 25

1. Heat 2 tablespoons of oil in a broad vessel and fry the cashewnuts until golden. Remove and keep aside. In the same oil, fry the semolina on a low heat until golden brown in colour. Keep aside.
2. In the same vessel, add the remaining oil and fry the vermicelli until golden brown in colour.
3. Mix the semolina, vermicelli, cashewnuts, curds, salt and enough water to form a batter of a dropping consistency.

For the tempering

1. Heat the oil and fry the dal and mustard seeds until they begin to crackle. Add the green chillies and curry leaves.
2. Add this mixture to the idli batter. Mix well.

How to proceed

Prepare the idlis by filling the batter in the cavities of an idli vessel and steaming.

▶ *Serve hot with coconut chutney* ◀

QUICK GREEN PEAS SNACK

This tasty dish can also be served along with the main meal.

Preparation time : 15 minutes. Cooking time : 10 minutes. Serves 4.

2 teacups tender green peas
1¼ level teaspoons
black pepper powder
½ teaspoon chilli powder
¼ teaspoon ginger powder
¼ teaspoon sugar
1 tablespoon butter
1 tablespoon amchur powder
½ teaspoon roasted
cumin seed powder
1 tablespoon
chopped coriander
2 tablespoons oil
salt to taste

For serving
papadis, page 106

1. Heat the oil on a tawa (griddle). Add the green peas, black pepper powder, chilli powder, ginger powder, sugar and salt and cook for 2 to 3 minutes.
2. Add the butter, amchur powder, cumin seed powder and toss.
3. Remove from the heat, sprinkle coriander and top with papadis.

▶ **Serve hot** ◀

SEMOLINA UTTAPA

An easy to-prepare version of the traditional uttapa.

Preparation time : 10 minutes. Cooking time : 20 minutes. Makes 10 to 12 uttapa.

1½ teacups semolina (sooji)
4 tablespoons fresh curds
1 tablespoon oil
salt to taste

§

For topping
3 tomatoes, sliced
3 onions, sliced
chilli powder
oil for cooking

For serving
coconut chutney, page 25

1. Mix the semolina, curds, salt and enough warm water to make a batter of a dropping consistency. Keep overnight.
2. Next day, add the oil and mix well.
3. Grease a tawa (griddle) with a little oil and heat.
Spread a little batter on the hot tawa, top with tomato and onion slices and sprinkle chilli powder and salt on top.
4. Pour a little oil on the sides and cook until brown on the underside.
Turn and cook on the other side. Repeat with the remaining batter.

▶ **Serve hot with coconut chutney** ◀

SPICY CHAAT–
CALCUTTA STYLE

Chat over this tasty chaat of fruits and vegetables.

Preparation time : 15 minutes. Cooking time : 30 minutes. Serves 6 to 8.

For the pakodis
175 grams black gram (urad) dal
75 grams moong dal
4 green chillies
12 mm. piece ginger
1 level teaspoon
nigella seeds (kalonji)
¼ level teaspoon asafoetida
salt to taste
oil for deep frying

For the papadis
250 grams plain
flour (maida)
2 level teaspoons
ajwain powder
1 tablespoon oil
salt to taste
oil for deep frying

For serving
2½ teacups fresh curds
2 potatoes, boiled and sliced
sweet chutney, page 24
green chutney, page 25
chaat masala, page 125
cumin seed powder
chilli powder
salt

For the pakodis
1. Soak the black gram dal and moong dal in water for 3 to 4 hours.
2. Drain, add the green chillies and ginger and blend in a mixer with a little water.
3. Add the nigella seeds, asafoetida and salt and mix.
4. Shape the mixture into small balls.
5. Deep fry in hot oil until golden brown.
6. Soak the fried pakodis in water for 30 minutes.
7. Squeeze out the water and keep aside.

For the papadis

1. Mix the flour, ajwain, oil and salt and add enough water to make a soft dough.
2. Knead well and roll out into small thin rounds of about 40 mm. diameter, without using flour if possible. Prick with a fork.
3. Deep fry in hot oil until golden brown.

How to proceed

1. Beat the curds with a little salt.
2. In each serving dish, place a few pakodis, some potato slices and a few papadis dipped in sweet chutney.
3. Sprinkle a little green chutney, curds, chaat masala, cumin seed powder, chilli powder and salt on top.

 Serve

MANPASAND MITHAI

(Sweets)

A large number of *desi* sweets are milk based.
Try Baked Bundi with Rabdi and Jhat-Pat
Halwa (made from just milk and curds) for
their unique taste. From Bengal, there are
Paneer and Coconut Balls, Orange Sandesh
and Mishti Doi. And from Gujarat are
somewhat different sweets like Gram Flour
Seera, Sweet Rice, Apple Rabdi and Nariyal
Ki Meethi Roti.

PANEER
And
COCONUT BALLS

Picture on page 112

This colourful sweet does not use any fat.

Preparation time : 20 minutes. Cooking time : 10 minutes. Makes 20 balls.

For the paneer balls
500 grams paneer, page 126
8 tablespoons powdered sugar
2 to 3 teaspoons rose water
a few drops rose essence

For the coconut mixture
3 teacups grated fresh coconut
1 ½ teacups granulated sugar
2 pinches saffron
a little milk

For decoration
4 to 5 blanched and chopped pistachios
silver foil

For the paneer balls
1. Mix all the ingredients very well and make a dough.
2. Divide the dough into 20 portions and shape into small round balls.

For the coconut mixture
1. Cook the coconut and sugar for 10 minutes on a slow flame. Cool.
2. Warm the saffron in a small vessel. Add a little milk and
rub in until the saffron dissolves.
3. Add the saffron mixture to the coconut mixture. Mix well.

How to proceed
1. Make a covering of the coconut mixture over each paneer ball using hand pressure.
2. Arrange the balls in a plate and cover with silver foil. Chill.
3. Cut each ball into 2 parts. Decorate with pistachios.

 ▶ **Serve cold** ◀

MALAI PEDAS

> *Traditional pedas made of khoya and sugar.*

Preparation time : 25 minutes. Cooking time : 50 minutes. Makes 18 pedas.

1 litre milk
100 grams sugar
2 pinches citric acid
2 pinches saffron
4 teaspoons milk
1 level teaspoon cornflour
4 to 5 cardamoms, powdered

For decoration

a few blanched and
chopped almonds
a few blanched and
chopped pistachios

1. Boil the milk in a broad vessel, stirring throughout until it becomes half in quantity.
2. Add the sugar and boil again for 4 to 5 minutes.
3. Mix the citric acid in 3 teaspoons of water. Add this mixture very gradually to the boiling milk until it curdles slightly. This may require anything from half to the entire quantity of the citric acid mixture.
4. Warm the saffron in a small vessel, add 2 teaspoons of milk and rub in until the saffron dissolves. Add to the boiling milk.
5. Mix the cornflour in 2 teaspoons of milk and add to the boiling milk.
6. Go on cooking and stirring till the mixture becomes thick.
7. Add the cardamom powder and mix well. Allow to cool.
8. Shape the mixture into 18 small balls.

▶ **Place in paper cups, decorate with the almonds and pistachios and serve** ◀

MALPUAS

Picture on page 111

> *Unlike the traditional deep-fried malpuas, these soft malpuas are only lightly fried.*

Preparation time : 20 minutes. Cooking time : 25 minutes. Serves 20.

For the syrup

1 teacup sugar
2 pinches saffron
2 teaspoons milk
2 teaspoons rose water (optional)

For the malpuas

200 grams fresh cream
4 tablespoons plain flour (maida)
1 teacup sugar
ghee for frying

For decoration
blanched and chopped almonds and pistachios

For the syrup
1. Dissolve the sugar in 1 teacup of water and boil for 5 minutes
to make a syrup of 1 thread consistency.
2. Warm the saffron in a small vessel, add the milk and rub until the saffron dissolves.
Add to the syrup.
3. Add the rose water. Keep the syrup warm.

How to proceed
1. Mix the cream and plain flour and prepare the batter.
2. Smear very little ghee on a frying pan and spread a small amount of the batter on it.
Fry on both sides using a little ghee.
3. Repeat with the rest of the batter.
4. Dip the malpuas in the hot sugar syrup. Decorate with almond and pistachio slices.

▶ *Serve hot* ◀

▶ **VARIATION: Spread the rabadi on top and serve.** ◀

ORANGE SANDESH

> *Tangy orange lends a special flavour to sandesh.*

Preparation time : 15 minutes. Cooking time : 10 minutes. Serves 6 to 8.

500 gms. paneer, page 126	**For decoration**
4 to 5 tablespoons (approx.)	segments of 2 oranges
powdered sugar	4 almonds,
1 teaspoon orange juice	blanched and sliced
2 drops orange essence (optional)	4 pistachios,
2 drops orange colour (optional)	blanched and sliced

1. Knead the paneer thoroughly with the sugar. Add the orange juice, orange essence
and orange colour and mix well. Spread half this mixture to form a 125 mm.
square on a plate or dish. Arrange half the orange segments on top.
2. Cover with the remaining paneer mixture, spreading it evenly on top Chill.

▶ **Decorate with the remaining orange segments, almonds and pistachios** ◀

SWEET RICE

An easy version of the traditional meetha chawal.

Preparation time : 10 minutes. Cooking time : 10 minutes. Serves 6.

4 teacups cooked rice
1 teacup sugar
2 tablespoons ghee
2 sticks cinnamon
2 cloves
2 bay leaves
2 pinches saffron

For decoration
a few blanched and sliced almonds and pistachios

1. Mix the rice and sugar.
2. Heat the ghee in a broad vessel and fry the cinnamon, cloves and bay leaves for a few seconds. Add the rice.
3. Warm the saffron in a small vessel, add 2 tablespoons of water and rub until it dissolves. Add to the rice.
4. Cook the rice on a slow flame until the sugar melts. Taste and add sugar if necessary. Decorate with almond and pistachio slices.

▶ **Serve hot** ◀

ALMOND-PISTACHIO ROLLS

Ideal for special occasions.

Preparation time : 20 minutes. Cooking time : 30 minutes. Makes 25 pieces.

For the pistachio dough
500 grams pistachios
250 grams sugar
2 pinches saffron
1/2 teaspoon cardamom powder

For the almond dough
1 kg. almonds
1 kg. sugar

For decoration
silver foil

Clockwise from top : Pistachio Baskets–Page 123 , Paneer Pistachio Rolls–Page 119,
Baked Bundi with Rabadi–Page 120, Paneer and Coconut Balls–Page 108

For the pistachio dough

1. Put the pistachios into boiling water for 4 to 5 minutes.
Drain, remove the skin by rubbing on a piece of cloth and grind into a powder.
2. Mix the sugar in 8 to 9 tablespoons of water and boil in a broad vessel until
it forms a soft ball. Add the pistachio powder and allow to cool.
3. Warm the saffron in a small vessel, add 2 teaspoons of milk
and rub until the saffron dissolves.
4. Add the saffron liquid and the cardamom powder to the pistachio dough.
5. Roll out the dough and make small rounds.

For the almond dough

1. Soak the almonds in water for 12 hours. Drain and put
into boiling water. Cover and leave for 10 minutes.
2. Drain the almonds, remove the skin and drop into cold water
so that they do not discolour.
3. Grind with a little water in a grinder. Add the sugar and cook until
the mixture forms into a dough. Leave for 5 minutes.

How to proceed

1. Roll out the almond dough and cut into square pieces which exactly cover
the pistachio rolls.
2. Place a pistachio roll on an almond square piece and roll up.
3. Repeat with the remaining pistachio and almond squares.

► *Decorate with silver foil, cut into small pieces and serve* ◄

DOUBLE DECKER SWEET

Colourful, light and tasty.

Preparation time : 15 minutes. Cooking time : 30 to 40 minutes. Serves 8 to 10.

2 tablespoons almonds
2 tablespoons pistachios
2 litres full fat milk
225 grams sugar
2 pinches powdered alum
2 pinches saffron
a little green colour

1. Put the almonds into hot water for 10 minutes.
Drain and remove the skin. Chop finely.
2. Chop the pistachios with the skin on very finely.
3. Put the milk in a large vessel, preferably in a non-stick pan, and heat on a high flame.
When it starts boiling, add the sugar and cook for 3 minutes.
4. Add the alum and continue boiling until the milk becomes very thick.
Test by putting a little mixture on a small plate.
If it forms a soft ball, remove from the heat.
5. Divide the mixture into two parts.
6. Warm the saffron in a small vessel, add 2 teaspoons of
milk and rub until the saffron dissolves.
7. Add the saffron liquid and almonds to 1 part of the milk mixture and mix well.
8. Add the pistachios and a few drops of green colour to the
other part of the milk mixture and mix well.
9. Grease a small plate and spread one part evenly over the surface.
Spread the other part on top. Store in a refrigerator.

▶ **Cut into pieces and serve** ◀

∽

MANGO VANILLA BARFI

You can either combine the two barfis as in this recipe or serve them separately.

Preparation time : 10 minutes. Cooking time : 20 minutes. Makes 10 to 12 pieces.

1 litre full fat milk.
150 grams sugar
a pinch alum powder
4 tablespoons mango juice (preferably Alphonso)
175 grams paneer, page 126
3 tablespoons sugar
½ teaspoon vanilla essence

For decoration
chopped almonds
chopped pistachios

1. Put the milk in a large vessel, preferably in a non-stick vessel, and boil on a high flame
2. When it starts boiling, add 150 grams of sugar. Boil again for 3 to 4 minutes on a high flame.
3. Add the alum powder and continue boiling and stirring until the mixture becomes thick.
4. Test by putting a little mixture on a small plate. If it forms a small ball, add the mango juice and continue cooking for at least 4 to 5 minutes.
5. Test once again by putting a little mixture on a small plate. If it forms a soft ball, remove from the heat and spread on a plate.
6. Crumble the paneer and knead well for 1 minute. Add 3 tablespoons of sugar and cook in a pan on a low heat for 2 to 3 minutes. Cool slightly and add the vanilla essence.
7. Spread this mixture over the mango mixture.
8. Sprinkle chopped nuts on top. Store in a refrigerator.

▶ **Cut into pieces and serve** ◀

KAJU – BARFI

A popular Indian sweet.

Preparation time : 15 minutes. Cooking time : 10 minutes. Makes 20 pieces.

500 grams cashewnuts
400 grams sugar
1 tablespoon rose water
a pinch saffron
a little milk
silver foil

1. Soak the cashewnuts in 1 litre of water for 2 to 4 hours.
2. Drain and grind them into a paste in a grinder.
3. Add the sugar and cook the mixture on a slow flame until of dough-like consistency. Add the rose water if the mixture is too hard.
4. Warm the saffron in a small vessel, add a little milk and rub until the saffron dissolves.
5. Cool the dough mixture slightly and add the saffron mixture. Mix very well.
6. Spread the mixture evenly on a smooth surface.
7. Spread the silver foil over it.

▶ **Cut into diamond shaped pieces and serve** ◀

APPLE RABADI

Apples help to thicken this tasty rabadi very quickly.

Preparation time : 5 minutes. Cooking time : 20 minutes. Serves 4 to 6.

1 litre full fat milk
4 tablespoons sugar
2 dessert apples
½ teaspoon cardamom powder
3 almonds, blanched and sliced

1. Put the milk in a broad vessel and boil.
2. Add the sugar and cook on a slow flame while stirring continuously,
until the mixture reduces to half.
3. Peel the apples and grate them. Add to the milk, give one boil and remove from the
heat at once. Sprinkle almonds and cardamom powder on top.

▶ **Serve hot** ◀

GRAM FLOUR SEERA

Delicious and easy to make.

Preparation time : 15 minutes. Cooking time : 20 minutes. Serves 6.

1 teacup gram flour (besan)
1 teacup milk
5 tablespoons melted ghee
¾ to 1 teacup sugar

2 pinches saffron (optional)
¼ teaspoon cardamom powder
5 to 6 almonds, blanched and sliced

1. Mix 2 tablespoons of the milk and 1 tablespoon of the ghee and add to the flour.
Rub into the mixture thoroughly and leave for 10 minutes.
2. Sieve the mixture using a coarse sieve.
3. Heat the remaining ghee in a broad vessel, add the flour mixture and cook
while stirring until slightly golden in colour.
4. In another vessel, mix 1 teacup of water and the balance milk.
Heat and add to the flour.
5. Add the sugar and continue cooking and stirring until the ghee separates.
6. Warm the saffron in a small vessel, add 2 teaspoons of milk and rub until
the saffron dissolves. Add to the flour mixture.
7. Put in a serving plate and sprinkle the cardamom powder and sliced almonds on top.

▶ **Serve hot** ◀

SAFFRON KULFI

> *A traditional kulfi.*

Preparation time : 15 minutes. Cooking time : 30 minutes. Serves 6 to 8.

2 litres full fat milk
1 level tablespoon cornflour
6 to 8 tablespoons sugar
10 almonds, blanched and chopped
15 pistachios, blanched and chopped
2 pinches saffron
½ teaspoon cardamom powder

1. Mix the milk, cornflour and sugar very well so that no lumps remain.
2. Put the mixture in a broad vessel and boil until it is reduced to 1/3 in volume. Cool.
3. Warm the saffron in a small vessel, add 2 teaspoons of milk and rub
   until the saffron dissolves.
4. Add the saffron liquid, chopped nuts and cardamom powder and mix very well.
5. Pour the mixture into small kulfi moulds and screw the lids tightly.
   Place in the freezer.
6. Just before serving, unmould and cut into slices.

▶ **Serve immediately** ◀

SWEET POTATO RABADI

> *Sweet potato blends temptingly into a rich rabadi.*

Preparation time : 5 minutes. Cooking time : 15 minutes. Serves 4 to 6.

1 litre full fat milk
2 sweet potatoes (200 grams), peeled and grated
150 grams sugar
2 pinches saffron
¼ teaspoon cardamom powder
2 almonds, blanched and sliced
2 pistachios, blanched and sliced

1. Put the milk to boil in a large vessel. Add the sweet potatoes and continue cooking until the potatoes are tender.
2. Add the sugar and continue cooking for 2 minutes. Remove from the heat.
3. Warm the saffron in a small vessel, add 2 teaspoons of milk and rub until the saffron dissolves.
4. Add the saffron liquid and the cardamom powder to the rabadi. Mix well and put to chill.
5. Just before serving, sprinkle the almonds and pistachios on top.

▶ **Serve cold** ◀

AGAR AGAR SWEET

Light and nutritious.

Preparation time : 5 minutes. Cooking time : 15 minutes. Serves 6.

6 teacups full fat milk
21 teaspoons sugar
12 teaspoons China grass
(agar agar), cut into small pieces

2 pinches saffron
½ teaspoon cardamom powder
2 almonds, blanched and sliced
2 pistachios, blanched and sliced
rose petals to decorate

1. Cook the China grass with 1 teacup of water on a slow flame until it melts.
2. Boil the milk with the sugar for at least 3 to 4 minutes.
3. Add the China grass mixture to the boiling milk and boil again for 3 minutes.
4. Strain the mixture.
5. Warm the saffron in a small vessel, add 2 teaspoons of milk and rub until the saffron dissolves.
6. Add the saffron liquid and the cardamom powder to the milk and pour into a flat serving dish. Put to set in the refrigerator.
7. Just before serving, decorate with rose petals, sliced almonds and pistachios.

▶ **Cut into pieces and serve cold** ◀

PANEER PISTACHIO ROLLS

Picture on page 112

Rich and tasty.

Preparation time : 10 minutes. No cooking. Makes 4 to 6 rolls.

100 grams crumbled paneer, page 126
4 teaspoons milk
2 tablespoons powdered sugar
2 tablespoons roasted ground pistachios
½ teaspoon cardamom powder
a few drops rose or kewra essence (optional)

For decoration
chopped nuts or silver foil

1. Knead the paneer, milk and sugar very well.
2. Add the pistachios, cardamom powder and essence.
3. Shape the paneer dough into small rolls.

► **Roll into chopped nuts or cover with silver foil** ◄

BAKED BUNDI

With

RABADI

Picture on page 112

Ideal for parties.

Preparation time : 20 minutes. Cooking time : 45 minutes. Serves 4 to 6.

For the bundi
1 teacup gram flour
(besan)
¾ teacup water
ghee for frying

For the rabadi
1 litre milk
100 grams sugar

For the sugar syrup for the bundi)
1 teacup sugar
¾ teacup water
2 pinches saffron

Other ingredients
2 cardamoms, powdered
a few blanched almonds, sliced

For the sugar syrup (for the bundi)
1. Mix the sugar and water and boil the mixture till it reaches 2 threads consistency.
2. Cool slightly.
3. Warm the saffron in a small vessel, add a little water and rub until the saffron dissolves. Add to the syrup.

For the bundi

1. Prepare a smooth batter with the gram flour and water.
2. Heat the ghee and pour the batter over a bundi jhara so that bundis drop
into the hot ghee. Fry the bundis.
3. Put the bundis in the hot sugar syrup and allow to soak the syrup for a few minutes.

For the rabadi

1. Put the milk to boil with the sugar stirring continously, until reduced to 2 cups.
2. Allow to cool slightly.

How to proceed

1. Just 15 minutes before serving, spread the bundi evenly in a baking dish.
2. Pour the rabadi mixture over it and sprinkle sliced almonds and
cardamom powder on top.
3. Bake in a hot oven at 200°C (400°F) for 15 minutes.

▶ *Serve hot or cold* ◀

▶ *Variation : BAKED BUNDI IN MANGO RABADI*
To the rabadi, add 3 to 4 tablespoons of mango pulp and proceed in the same way. ◀

JHAT-PAT HALWA

Quick and nutritous.

Preparation time : 10 minutes. Cooking time : 20 minutes. Serves 4.

1 litre milk
100 grams sugar
2 tablespoons fresh curds
2 pinches saffron
2 cardamoms, powdered

For decoration

chopped pistachios
chopped almonds

1. Mix the milk, sugar and curds and put to boil in a broad vessel.
Go on heating and stirring until the mixture becomes thick.
2. Warm the saffron in a small vessel, add a little warm milk and
rub until the saffron dissolves.
3. Add the saffron liquid and cardamon powder to the milk mixture.

▶ *Sprinkle the chopped pistachios and almonds on top and serve* ◀

NARIYAL KI MEETHI ROTI

Nutmeg gives a special flavour to this sweet roti.

Preparation time : 20 minutes. Cooking time : 30 minutes. Makes about 10 rotis.

For the dough
3 teacups whole wheat flour
1 tablespoon melted ghee
salt to taste

For the stuffing
1 teacup grated fresh coconut
1 teacup powdered sugar
½ teaspoon cardamom powder
½ teaspoon nutmeg (jaiphal) powder
2 teaspoons ghee

For cooking
ghee

For the dough
1. Sieve the flour with the salt.
2. Add the ghee and mix very well.
3. Add enough water and make a soft dough.

For the stuffing
1. Melt the ghee and add the coconut. Cook on a slow flame, stirring continuously until it is lightly coloured and totally dry. This should takes about 15-20 minutes. Cool.
2. When cool, add the sugar, cardamom powder and nutmeg powder and mix well. Taste and add extra sugar and nutmeg as desired.

How to proceed
1. Knead the dough and divide into 20 portions.
2. Roll out each portion of the dough into a small round of about 100 mm. diameter.
3. Spread 1 tablespoon of the stuffing on one round and dampen the edges by applying water. Press another round on top and seal the edges to enclose the stuffing completely. Repeat for the remaining rounds and stuffing.
4. Cook on a hot tawa (griddle) on both sides using a little ghee until pink spots come on top.

▶ **Serve hot** ◀

PISTACHIO BASKETS

Picture on page 112

A novel form of pista barfi with tasty filling.

Preparation time : 15 minutes. Cooking time : 25 minutes. Makes 15 pieces.

For the pistachio baskets
250 grams pistachios
125 grams sugar

To be mixed into a filling
100 grams crumbled paneer, page 126
3 tablespoons fresh cream
3 tablespoons powdered sugar

For the pistachio baskets
1. Put the pistachios into boiling water for 4 to 5 minutes.
2. Drain, remove the skin by rubbing on a piece of cloth and grind into a powder.
3. Mix the sugar in 4 to 5 tablespoons of water and boil in a broad vessel
until 2 threads consistency is achieved.
Check the right consistency by dropping a few drops of syrup into cold water.
It should form a soft ball when rolled between your fingers.
4. Add the pistachio powder, mix well and allow to cool.
5. Roll out the pistachio dough and press into desired moulds.
6. Store in a refrigerator.

How to proceed
Unmould the pistachio baskets and fill a teaspoonful of the filling in each basket.

▶ **Serve** ◀

MISHTI DOI

Picture on page 27

Bengal's famous sweet curds.

Preparation time : 15 minutes. Cooking time : 15 minutes. Serves 8.

1 litre full fat milk
200 grams sugar
2 teaspoons sweet curds

1. Add 125 grams of sugar to the milk and put to boil on a high flame for 10 minutes.
2. Place the remaining 75 grams of sugar in heavy bottom vessel with 2 tablespoons of water and melt on a slow flame. Allow the mixture to become dark brown in colour.
3. Gradually add this sugar mixture to the boiled milk and boil again for 5 minutes.
4. Cool the mixture to lukewarm. Add the curds and mix well.
5. Cover and allow to set for 6 to 8 hours.
6. Store in a refrigerator.

NOTE : Increase the quantity of sweet curds from 2 to 3 teaspoons in the hot season.

BASIC RECIPES

FRESH GARAM MASALA

Preparation time : a few minutes. Cooking time : 2 to 3 minutes. Makes about 2 tablespoons.

2 sticks cinnamon
2 cloves
1 bay leaf
2 peppercorns
½ teaspoon cumin seeds
½ teaspoon coriander seeds

1. Roast all the ingredients in a heavy based pan or tawa (griddle) on a very slow flame
until the spices release their aroma. Cool.
2. Grind into a powder and store in an air-tight container.

▶ **Use as required** ◀

CHAAT MASALA

Preparation time : a few minutes. No cooking. Makes 5 teacups.

1 teacup slightly roasted   1 teacup amchur powder
coriander seeds   2 tablespoons black pepper
1 teacup red chillies   1 teacup salt
1 teacup roasted cumin seeds   2. tablespoons black salt (sanchal)

1. Powder all the ingredients together.
2. Store in an air-tight container.

▶ **Use as required** ◀

PANEER

Preparation time : 10 minutes. Cooking time : 10 minutes. Makes about 350 grams.

2 litres milk
juice of 2 lemons

1. Put the milk to boil. When it starts boiling, add the lemon juice. Remove from the heat and stir gently until the milk curdles and bluish water floats on top.
2. Strain. Tie the curdled milk in a muslin cloth and hang for at least 2 hours to allow the water to drain out.

▶ **Use as required** ◀

PUNJABI GARAM MASALA

Preparation time : 15 minutes. No cooking. Makes 2 cups.

100 grams cumin seeds	15 grams cinnamon
75 grams cardamom seeds	20 grams mace (optional)
65 grams peppercorn	20 grams black cumin seeds
35 grams coriander seeds	15 grams bay leaves
35 grams fennel (saunf) seeds	15 grams ginger powder
20 grams cloves	3 nutmeg (Jaiphal)

1. Grind all the ingredients except ginger powder to a fine powder in a grinder.
2. Add the ginger powder and mix well.
3. Sieve and store in an air-tight container.

▶ **Use as required** ◀